Grateful

GIVING THANKS TO GOD
IN ALL THINGS

LIFEWAY WOMEN

Lifeway Press®
Brentwood, Tennessee

Published by Lifeway Press® • © 2023 Lifeway Christian Resources •
Brentwood, TN

ISBN: 978-1-0877-7980-5
Item: 005841132
Dewey decimal classification: 248.843

Subject headings: GRATITUDE \ WOMEN \ CHRISTIAN LIFE

Unless indicated otherwise, all Scripture taken from the Christian
Standard Bible®, Copyright © 2020 by Holman Bible Publishers.
Used by permission. Christian Standard Bible® and CSB® are
federally registered trademarks of Holman Bible Publishers.
Scripture quotations are from the ESV® Bible (The Holy Bible,
English Standard Version®), copyright © 2001 by Crossway, a
publishing ministry of Good News Publishers. Used by permission.
All rights reserved. Scriptures taken from the Holy Bible, New
International Version®, NIV®. Copyright © 1973, 1978, 1984, 2011 by
Biblica, Inc.™ Used by permission of Zondervan. All rights reserved
worldwide. zondervan.com The "NIV" and "New International
Version" are trademarks registered in the United States Patent and
Trademark Office by Biblica, Inc.®

To order additional copies of this resource, write to Lifeway
Resources Customer Service; 200 Powell Place, Suite 100,
Brentwood, TN 37027-7707; order online at lifeway.com;
fax 615.251.5933; phone toll free 800.458.2772; or email
orderentry@lifeway.com.

Printed in the United States of America

Lifeway Women Bible Studies • Lifeway Resources •
200 Powell Place, Suite 100, Brentwood, TN 37027-7707

EDITORIAL TEAM, LIFEWAY WOMEN BIBLE STUDIES

Becky Loyd
Director,
Lifeway Women

Tina Boesch
Manager

Chelsea Waack
Production Leader

Mike Wakefield
Content Editor

Laura Magness
Managing Editor

Tessa Morrell
Production Editor

Lauren Ervin
Art Director

Sarah Hobbs
Graphic Designer

CONTENTS

How to
USE THIS STUDY

Welcome to _Grateful: Giving Thanks to God in All Things._ We pray this study fosters in you a heart of gratitude regardless of what time of year you choose to do it. We hope you'll find being grateful turns your eyes off yourself and helps you cherish your time and relationships in a new way. When we are a thankful people, we point to our good God who loves and provides for us.

GETTING STARTED

Because we believe discipleship happens best in community, we encourage you to do this study together in a group setting. Or, if you're doing this alone, consider enlisting a friend or two to go through it at the same time. This will give you study friends to pray with and connect with over coffee or through text or email so you can chat about what you're learning.

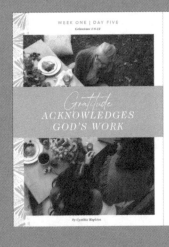

PERSONAL STUDY

The five days of personal study each week will feature a profile of someone in the Bible who portrayed a grateful heart, two days of teaching from Scripture on gratefulness, one psalm of thanksgiving, and a day to practice being grateful.

REFLECTION PAGE

At the end of each week, you'll find a page for you to reflect on what you've experienced in the previous days of study. There's space for you to journal, write a poem or song, draw, or whatever best expresses your heart of gratitude.

LEADING A GROUP?

A free leader guide PDF is available for download at lifeway.com/grateful. The leader guide offers several tips and helps, along with discussion guides for each week.

FREE DOWNLOADS

Resources are available to help you promote the study in your church or neighborhood, including: invitation card, promotional poster, bulletin insert, and PowerPoint® template. You'll find these and more at lifeway.com/grateful.

INTRODUCTION

Say thank you!

Did you say thank you?

I've got to write my thank you notes!

Thank you, thank you, thank you.

From the moment toddlers learn to speak, we are teaching them to say thank you. This lesson in manners is hopefully something we all carry through the rest of our lives, intentionally voicing gratitude for what people do for us or give us. Depending on the country you live in, you may even have a national holiday set aside to remember to be thankful. But those are moments—circumstances, calendar dates, a feeling of "thankfulness" when good things happen.

Throughout the Bible, gratefulness is seen as a permanent characteristic of the people of God, not a temporary feeling. The apostle Paul said those who follow Christ are to be "overflowing with gratitude" (Col. 2:7b). But did he mean all the time? Even in suffering, hardship, and loss? Yes. In those times too. How do we reconcile this? How do we learn to be women who feel grateful even when our circumstances don't seem to warrant it?

Harvard Health Publishing released an article titled "Giving thanks can make you happier." In it, they shared the following from a research study on gratitude:

Two psychologists, Dr. Robert A. Emmons of the University of California, Davis, and Dr. Michael E. McCullough of the University of Miami, have done much of the research on gratitude. In one study, they asked all participants to write a few sentences each week, focusing on particular topics.

One group wrote about things they were grateful for that had occurred during the week. A second group wrote about daily irritations or things that had displeased them, and the third wrote about events that had affected them (with no emphasis on them being positive or negative). After ten weeks, those who wrote about gratitude were more optimistic and felt better about their lives. Surprisingly, they also exercised more and had fewer visits to physicians than those who focused on sources of aggravation.[1]

It seems (and I imagine this won't surprise you) that gratitude begins in what our thoughts dwell on. As women of God, do we actively think about Him and the promises and blessings the Bible tells us are ours as followers of Jesus? Or do we spend our time comparing ourselves to others—envying the perfect lives we see presented to us through social media feeds and bemoaning our daily grind or challenging relationships? Because to be women who overflow with gratitude as God's Word tells us to be, we can't do both.

Over the next four weeks, we'll live in this gratitude tension as we dig into Scripture together.

To write this study, we've brought together a team of godly, gifted women from many different seasons of life who have lived through a wide range of experiences. The wisdom they've gained through years of walking with the Lord has stretched their understanding of what it means to be grateful to God in all things.

What we hope you'll take away from this Bible study is that God created you, saved you, loves you, and is using you for His good purpose—to glorify Him and extend His love to others. So, no matter how your life measures up against those around you or how hard things get from time to time, a heart of gratitude is possible simply because of who Jesus is and who you are in Him.

We're thrilled you're spending the next four weeks with us. Our prayer is that we will be women who learn to "rejoice always, pray constantly, give thanks in everything; for this is God's will for you in Christ Jesus" (1 Thess. 5:15-18).

Laura Magness

WEEK ONE

A grateful heart flows out of an understanding of who Jesus is and who we are in Him. When we are rightly oriented before God the Father—our Creator and Redeemer—we are never without things to be thankful for. No matter the ebbs and flows of our circumstances, our identity as His daughters doesn't change. The Bible passages we'll study this week include a Gospel story and two important teachings that show us if the only thing we have to be grateful for is new life in Jesus, that's enough for our hearts to overflow with gratitude every day.

THE *Gratitude* OF ONE

by Wendy Bello

There was a time in my life when gratitude was more of a foreign concept. Yes, I understood what the word meant, and giving thanks to others as a social convention was something my parents and grandparents instilled in me. But I didn't live with a grateful heart. Then one day the Lord used a book I was reading to reveal how the sin of ungratefulness had taken root in my life and how quickly I'd forgotten the wonderful things He had done.

Remembering God's goodness and mercies inevitably produces gratitude, but we have forgetful hearts. Just like many of the characters in today's story.

READ LUKE 17:11-13.

This passage is part of a large section in the gospel of Luke that narrates Jesus's journey to Jerusalem (Luke 9:51–19:41). While on the way, Jesus had an encounter with a group of men who suffered from leprosy. *Leprosy* was a general term used for different acute skin conditions. The law of Moses required that lepers live outside the city (Num. 5:2-4) and not be allowed to mingle with the rest of the people. As they went about, they were to cover their mouths and cry out "Unclean, unclean" (Lev. 13:45-46). Therefore, when this group of men saw Jesus coming, they kept their distance and raised their voices so He could hear them.

> What was their plea to Jesus? Why do you think they asked this of Jesus?

> How would you have felt if you had been part of this group of people?

Sometimes we can feel like these men: outcasts, excluded, alone. We're not forced to live outside our towns or cities, but sometimes we choose to keep our distance from others and even from the Lord. Maybe we separate ourselves because of sin or shame, or perhaps we're confused or afraid. But let's be encouraged by this text. Like these men, we can call on the name of the Lord. He is a merciful God! But what exactly does that mean?

How would you define God's mercy?

One theologian defined *God's mercy* as "the goodness or love of God shown to those who are in misery or distress, irrespective of their deserts."[1] Receiving His mercy does not depend on our merits or behavior. We can't do anything to win His mercy. It is His prerogative. And here's something amazing about God's mercy: it never runs out! There is an unlimited supply. In fact, Scripture tells us God's mercies are new every morning (Lam. 3:22-23).

Describe a time when you experienced God's mercy. What impact did it have in your life?

READ LUKE 17:14-16.

The law commanded that a person afflicted with any skin disease had to be examined by a priest. This examination would determine if the person was clean or not. If clean, the person was allowed to return to a normal life with the rest of the people (Lev. 14:2-32).

IN LUKE 5:12-13, Jesus had an earlier encounter with a leprous man. Read the passage and compare it to the Luke 17 encounter. What differences do you find?

When Jesus commanded the men in chapter 17 to go show themselves to the priests, they were still sick and unclean. Their healing took place while they were on the way to the priests. Can you imagine the amazement those men felt when they looked at their bodies and saw no traces of leprosy? Jesus hadn't even touched them, yet they witnessed the power of the one true God!

The faith and obedience of the ten were also involved in the process. They had faith in what Jesus said and obeyed His command. That should be the case in our walk with the Lord. The old hymn rings true:

Trust and obey, for there's no other way

to be happy in Jesus, but to trust and obey.[2]

TRUST AND OBEY

After the healing took place, Luke notes that one of the men returned praising God.

What do we learn from the text about the identity of this man? Why is that important?

The text emphasizes the nationality of one man, the Samaritan. Samaritans and Jews were not on friendly terms. The Jews despised the Samaritans and considered them unclean. The groups had a long history of racial and religious conflict. But it was the Samaritan leper who came back with a grateful heart. The mercy of Jesus had changed his life, and he could not remain silent. He returned shouting and praising God.

Can you recall a time in your life when you had been praying about something for a long time and suddenly the Lord answered? Describe the experience.

Did you come back to thank Him like the Samaritan, or did you just go on your way like the other nine lepers?

As we noted earlier, sometimes our hearts have memory problems. Too easily we go on with our lives and forget to thank the Lord for the many occasions He has been merciful to us.

READ LUKE 17:17-19.

It's interesting that Jesus asked about the other nine lepers who were cleansed. After all, He had told them to go see the priest and they had obeyed. But it seems as if He expected them all to come back.

Why would Jesus ask this?

READ VERSE 18 AGAIN. Jesus made a connection between gratitude and giving God glory. Remember when I told you earlier about my own ungrateful heart? Well, my journey also included reading through the Bible and learning what gratitude really means. One verse from Psalms was an eye-opener, "The one who offers thanksgiving as his sacrifice glorifies me" (Ps. 50:23, ESV). Giving thanks to God is honoring Him, a way of glorifying Him as we acknowledge what He has done. When we realize how merciful the Lord has been to us and the magnitude of our salvation, giving thanks should be the natural response of the heart. Jesus was bringing that to the attention not only of the cleansed Samaritan but also of His disciples who were watching the episode unfold.

The ten lepers came to Jesus looking for healing, but the last verse reveals that the Samaritan received more than he asked for. Jesus told the man "Your faith has saved you" (". . . has made you well" ESV, NIV). The Greek word for *saved* is *sozo*, a word used in the New Testament to speak of salvation from sin.[3] His healing went beyond the physical realm. The power of Jesus not only transformed his body but also his heart.

Take an honest look at your own heart. Would you say that your life is a sacrifice of thanksgiving that gives God the glory? When was the last time you took a moment to reflect on God's mercy and give Him thanks? Use the space below to write a prayer of gratitude to the Lord. Also pray that He would help you live a life of thanksgiving.

Jesus MEETS WITH NICODEMUS

by April Rodgers

I magine you are placed in a large darkened room, filled with obstacles. You're told to find a different way out than the way you entered. You extend your hands as you stumble around, desperately trying to find the exit. Panic begins to creep in the longer you search. But all of a sudden, light illuminates the room, and you are able to clearly see the other exit and the path to get there.

Sometimes, studying the Scripture can feel a little like finding our way through the darkened room. But God has given us His Spirit to lead us into all truth. Let's pray that the eyes of our hearts are enlightened today to receive the lesson the Spirit has for us. And who better to teach us than the ultimate Teacher Himself? Just as Jesus took the time to explain the mystery of salvation to Nicodemus, the same opportunity is extended to us. Let's pull up a chair at the table of gratitude and learn from the Master.

> READ JOHN 3:1-21 and pay extra attention to these repeated words: *born, Spirit, believe, light.*

Nicodemus was an important man. A Pharisee. A ruler of the Jews. A man of prestige and authority. A man with many years of dedicated time spent studying the Scriptures and teaching them to others. Yet he came to Jesus seeking answers and desiring to know more. He knew that Jesus was a miracle-worker, but Nicodemus would come to know Jesus as much more than that. As Jesus began to unveil who He truly was and His purpose for coming to earth, Nicodemus struggled to comprehend. His earthly eyes were keeping him in the dark.

> Have you ever desired to know the deep things of God, but when you opened your Bible, what you found felt foreign or confusing to you? Explain.

Did the "light" ever come on so that you could discern what God's Word was saying? Explain.

As Jesus patiently explained the process of salvation to Nicodemus, He used the term *born again*. Nicodemus struggled to understand because he knew in the natural realm, this concept was impossible. But if we dig a little deeper, we discover this phrase *born again* can also be translated born *from above*.[4] Jesus went on to talk about this new birth in a different way.

How did Jesus describe the new birth in verse 5?

Jesus was not talking about two separate events of being born of water and of the Spirit, but a combining of two things to bring about spiritual birth. We see this described by the Old Testament prophets.

> For I will pour water on the thirsty land
>
> and streams on the dry ground;
>
> I will pour out my Spirit on your descendants
>
> and my blessing on your offspring.
>
> *ISAIAH 44:3*

This concept is especially clear in Ezekiel 36:25-27. Read it and summarize how the new birth was described.

READ 2 CORINTHIANS 5:17. How did Paul describe what takes place when we're born again?

Sounds wonderful, doesn't it? Who wouldn't want the old and crusty parts to be gone and to receive a new and fresh life? Yet to be born from above requires trust. We must believe that Jesus is who God says He is.

READ BACK OVER JOHN 3:14-18 and answer the following questions.

What is Jesus's relationship to God the Father, and what was His mission on earth?

What is the repeated action verb in this passage?

What are we given if we believe Jesus is God's Son?

Belief is a big deal to God. It's not just enough for us to acknowledge that Jesus was a good teacher or a miracle worker. God wants us to find Him trustworthy and in turn, place our complete faith in Him. God's desire is that His free gift of salvation be accepted by us and not tossed to the side in search of the next best thing. He wants us to know just how deeply He loves us because at the core of it all, love has always been the motivation.

When I was a little girl, I loved to play with Barbie® dolls, dressing them in the fanciest dresses and shoes. My best friend had a Barbie Dreamhouse® with an elevator that could move Barbie from the first floor to the second, and I thought that was the most magnificent thing. I wanted one of my own. So I asked my parents for my own Barbie Dreamhouse for Christmas. My father worked many nights in the garage long after I had gone to bed to build me a Barbie home from real wood, lining the walls with scraps of elegant wallpaper and giving Barbie plush carpet to rest her high-arched feet after a busy day of dress up.

When Christmas morning finally arrived, I rushed into the living room hoping to see the gift my heart desired, yet instead of the Mattel® Dreamhouse, there stood my father's creation. I was devastated to find that Barbie's home did not have an elevator or even stairs. How was she supposed to move from room to room unless I moved her (gasp!)? My eyes couldn't see the beautiful gift that was in front of me and how it was ten times better than the cheap plastic alternative. I'm sure it crushed my father to watch me reject his gift made with love because I longed for something inferior.

Our heavenly Father has given us a priceless gift. For God so loved you and me that He gave His only Son in order to rescue us from a life of darkness and sin. But ultimately, we have to decide to believe in Jesus. The gift of eternal life has been given. The question is this: will we receive it?

Friend, if you have never put your faith in Jesus Christ as your Lord and Savior, today is the day. Repent of your sins and believe in Him. Allow Him to breathe new life into you and make your spirit come alive as a new creation. Accept His free gift of love and eternal life. (For more information and guidance on this decision, see "Becoming a Christian" on page 141.)

Write out your response to His gift below.

If you have already received Jesus as the Son of God, write out a prayer of gratitude for all that He has done for you. Ask Him to strengthen and grow your belief in Him as you find Him trustworthy all over again.

In the end, Nicodemus brought his own gift to Jesus. John records that Nicodemus assisted Joseph of Arimathea in taking Jesus's body off the cross and placing Him in the garden tomb (John 19:38-42). As he anointed the body of the Son of God with myrrh and aloes, I wonder if Nicodemus reflected on their earlier all-important conversation, where being "born again" seemed impossible. What Nicodemus would soon discover is that nothing is impossible with God! For in three days' time, Light would once again break through the darkness as Jesus rose from the grave. At the core of it all, love was the motivation. For that, we can be truly grateful.

FOR HIS *Hesed* ENDURES FOREVER

by Irene Sun

"**H**is name is Khesed," I said as I smiled at the labor and delivery nurse, a tall and kind woman with gray hair. She was stationed in the nursery.

"What does it mean?" she asked.

"*Khesed*, or *hesed*, means *steadfast love* in Hebrew," I explained while she gently transferred my newborn into my arms. The crying stopped immediately.

Puzzled, the nurse responded, "I am Jewish, and the word for *love* in Hebrew is *ahav*."

She was right. *Hesed* is not love, not in the normal sense. *Hesed* is different. More than a feeling, *hesed* is an act.[5]

READ PSALM 136 WITH THESE QUESTIONS IN MIND.

1	Why do we give thanks?
2-3	Why is He who He is?
4-9	Why did He create the universe?
10-16	Why did He deliver His people?
17-22	Why did He provide a home to His people?
23-25	Why does He remember us now?
26	Why do we give thanks?

The resounding answer from beginning to end is: His faithful love endures forever. In Hebrew, the repeated phrase is made of two words, *olam* ("for to eternity") and *hesed*. Due to the depth and vastness of *hesed*, different Bible translations render *hesed* differently.

CSB: His **FAITHFUL LOVE** endures forever

KJV: for his **MERCY** endureth for ever

ESV: for his **STEADFAST LOVE** endures forever

NIV: His **LOVE** endures forever

In Scripture, here are four distinct features of *hesed*:

* *Hesed* is an act of faith, based on an established promise, a fulfillment of a covenant.

* *Hesed* responds to an urgent need of those who receive it.

* *Hesed* is a saving act toward a life that hangs on another person's mercy.

* *Hesed* is a free and extraordinary act of generosity.

Hesed is God's life-giving, unchanging, saving love. He does not "love us to death." He loves us to life.

Rahab and the two spies in Joshua 2:12, for example, promised to show each other *hesed*. They made promises to each other to save one another's lives: "Our lives for yours" even to death! (Josh. 2:14). They were strangers to one another. They did not have prior feelings of love for each other. They were doing *hesed* on the basis of an established promise. They were fulfilling their vows when they saved each other's lives and responded to an urgent need.

Hesed is the foundation for why God creates and the reason for why He saves. *Hesed* sets Yahweh apart from all other gods. It is at the core of His character. He is a God who keeps His word. He not only desires to save, He is able to save. Infinite love with infinite power. There is no one like Him.

What is the effect of having the chorus repeated in every other line?

Salvation, in this psalm and in the entirety of Scripture, is not merely to be saved from death. God's people are saved unto God, to be in relationship with Him. Yahweh is the destination of our salvation. If we don't want Yahweh, we don't want salvation. *Jesus*, or *Yeshua*, means *salvation* in Hebrew.

There is no God like Yahweh. He is the God of gods. He is the Lord of lords. He is set apart from all the other idols because of His goodness. Psalm 136 recounts the ways God displays His goodness.

By what means did God create the universe (vv. 4-9)?

Notice how Yahweh *alone* does great works. Yahweh *alone* created the great wonders. Not by might nor by power but by His understanding. Yahweh is not a human being, but He is a person and He has a mind. In the ancient world, inanimate objects in nature such as stone, wood, and metal were worshiped. Unlike these false gods, Yahweh created great wonders—the earth, sea, and stars—by speaking words.

In verses 10-16, the psalmist recounts God's deliverance of His people from the shackles of slavery. Why did He do this? Because of His faithful, steadfast, and forever love. The deliverance of God's people was established on God's promise to Abraham, a fulfillment of a covenant. The need was urgent as Pharaoh was killing the baby boys and God's people cried out in misery. The exodus was extraordinarily generous, accomplished for a people who were ungrateful and often complaining. They even accused God of killing them.

Then in verses 17-22 we see that not only did God deliver His people, but He provided a place for them, a promised land.

How does the death of these kings show the *hesed* of Yahweh?

Back in Genesis 15, God made a covenant with Abram. Not only would Abram have offspring (he was childless at the time), but his offspring would inherit a land. God fulfilled His promises when He struck down the kings who were occupying the land and gave the land to Israel as a heritage.

The psalmist snaps us back into the present in verses 23-25. Yahweh remembers us here and now. Presently, we are low and discouraged. Presently, we have enemies from whom we need to be rescued. Presently, we are fleshly creatures who need food. Even here and even now, His steadfast love endures forever.

In verse 26, the psalm ends exactly the way it began, by giving thanks. This is a literary device called an "inclusio." *Hesed* is an act we are able to do for another human, and it is an act that God can show to us, but we cannot show *hesed* to God. God is in need of nothing, and His life is never in danger. But in His kindness, He gives us the dignity to respond to His love by giving thanks.

List five good things that happened that brought you to Yahweh.

List five hard things that happened that brought you to Yahweh.

Speak each of those things aloud, repeating the chorus "His faithful love endures forever" after each one.

As said before, Yahweh is the destination of our salvation. We are not saved merely from danger, but we are saved to be with Him. We are saved to have a relationship with our Creator. We are saved to be in communion with our Savior and Friend.

He is consistent, unchanging, and worthy of our trust. He is the same yesterday, today, and forever. He saved us. He is saving us. He will save us. Because of *hesed*.

Alive WITH CHRIST

by Christina Zimmerman

The year before my dad died, he quietly told me that he would not be living next year. I responded with a nod and an attempt to reassure him that he would be okay. But he knew better. The diabetes and high blood pressure that wreaked havoc in his body dictated hopeless outcomes to his mind. He accepted those outcomes, but I did not. My father believed in Christ and knew where he was going after death, but I wanted my father to live.

At that time, I had yet to learn what Paul taught in the book of Ephesians about the death to life power available for all who trust in Christ. As a believer, my earthly father knew the resurrection power of God both in the present and in the future. Paul prayed that every Christian would know this power (Eph. 1:17-23). Then he explained simply and beautifully how that death to life transformation takes place.

READ EPHESIANS 2:1-3.

Paul's letter to the Ephesians provides readers with a bird's-eye view of God's grace at work in humanity. It shows that through Christ's death, burial, and resurrection we have been redeemed of past, present, and future sins. Also, Paul made clear what we were before we came to Christ, what we have in the present, and what we will have in the future.

In verses 1-3, Paul described the way we walked in the world before Jesus came into our hearts. In verse 1, he said we were dead in trespasses and sins. Before you became a Christian, you may have experienced many difficult circumstances— financial, physical, or relational. But the greatest adversity in your life at that time was that you were dead. Your body may have been alive, but you were spiritually dead. This made you dead to God. Ephesians 4:18 describes our state before Christ, "They are darkened in their understanding, excluded from the life of God."

In verse 2, Paul described us as following the ways of the world. Not only were we spiritually dead, but we were walking and living in sin. Without Christ, we were living in the realm of Satan, "the ruler of the power of the air," who influenced us to walk contrary to the ways of God. We lived according to our own sinful desires (v. 3).

Describe your life before you became a believer. Include how you viewed God, the church, and Christians at that time. If it's difficult for you to remember that because you came to Christ as a child, describe what prompted you to turn to Him.

How would your past have shaped your life if you had not become a believer and follower of Christ?

Paul presented a convincing case about people: we are dead in our sin without Christ, we cannot earn salvation on our own, and we deserve the wrath of God.

READ EPHESIANS 2:4-7. What all did Paul say God has done for us?

What motivated God to act on our behalf?

Verses 1-3 present a description of our dark and hopeless past. "But God" (v. 4) intervened into our hopeless and sinful condition. Paul shared that God, who is "rich in mercy," made us alive. He did this "because of His great love . . . for us" (v. 4). We deserved God's wrath, but "For God so loved" (John 3:16, ESV) came to fruition. That's the miracle of salvation.

The same power that raised Christ from the dead has made us spiritually alive. Because we have been granted a new spiritual life, we can have a relationship with God. We can know Him intimately. We can read the Bible and understand what God is saying to us.

> What else changed in your life and thinking when you were made spiritually alive? What has been the benefit of these changes? (See vv. 6-7 to help with your answer.)

In verse 6, Paul seemed to build in crescendo the blessings of salvation. He stated that we have been raised together with Christ; that is, we have been united with Christ in His resurrected life. God also has "seated us with him in the heavens" (v. 6). Paul wanted believers to know that our citizenship is in heaven (Phil. 3:20). We are not there physically yet, but we are spiritually. We're no longer of this world; we are with Christ, even now. And because we are joined to Christ, what is true of Him is true of us. Paul wanted us to know that the benefits of being alive in Christ are not just something we look forward to in the future but something we enjoy now—blessing, security, honor, and responsibility.[6]

> Describe the joy you feel because of your eternal relationship with Christ.

READ EPHESIANS 2:8-10. Rewrite these verses in your own words.

In verses 8-10, Paul focused on three themes: grace, salvation, and faith.

GRACE. Paul used the word *grace* twelve times in Ephesians. In Paul's day, it meant pleasantness, favor, or gratitude.[7] However, it received new significance for Christians. The word was used here to describe the utter generosity God showed to sinners even though we didn't (and still don't) deserve it.

SALVATION. Paul used the word "saved" in these verses to refer to the various aspects of our salvation. He used it to indicate the salvation that was accomplished in the past continues to impact our lives in the present. In other words, salvation is a permanent condition. And, as Paul emphasized in verse 8-9, salvation is not something given because of good works. It is not an accomplishment; it is a gift.

FAITH. This word refers to a total openness to receiving God and the benefits of salvation into our lives. We trustfully accept what God has provided.[8] Our faith does not save us. God's grace saves us. Faith is the means by which we receive His grace.[9]

Finally, God has a purpose for saving us. We are His workmanship (v. 10). We are a work of art that God is in the process of designing. Day-by-day, He is changing us into the image of His dear Son. And because Christ came to serve, we are being made new to serve God and to serve others. This has been God's plan for us from the beginning. God's transforming grace will increasingly result in our doing works that are pleasing to Him.

How would you explain Ephesians 2:1-10 to a friend who doesn't know Jesus? What would be your talking points?

All the glory for our salvation goes to God. We were born spiritually dead into a sinful world, destined to spend eternity separated from the God who loves us. But God who is rich in grace sent His Son to be punished in our place. This truth should move us to live lives of gratefulness, extending thanks to God not just with our words but by the way we live. It is the right response for all God has done.

Gratitude
ACKNOWLEDGES GOD'S WORK

by Cynthia Hopkins

Zero percent of women who have looked at the cover of this study did so thinking, *I just don't know if gratitude is really all that important.* Granted, no poll or survey was conducted to confirm that statistic, but it has to be accurate, right? After all, the importance of gratitude is a generally accepted global truth. An internet search of quotes about gratitude proves this is true—Christians, Hindus, Jews, Universalists, Mormons, Muslims, Buddhists, and even atheists seek to identify reasons to be grateful. In every language, one of the first things parents teach children to say is "Thank you." Millions of viewers tune into annual award ceremonies to find out who will be awarded and how they will express gratitude. Stadiums full of sports fans spontaneously explode with applause and shouts of appreciation when athletes excel.

Gratitude is *nice*. We all know that; it's why we gather together as families at Thanksgiving. "Friendsgiving" has become a popular practice, too. That's not because we like turkey so much that we want to eat it oven-roasted on Thursday with our families and then deep-fried on Friday with our closest friends. No, it is simply because we like gratitude *that* much.

> So, if gratitude is a universally accepted value, then why do we need encouragement to embrace and practice that value?

The fact is, as much as we value gratitude, we struggle to practice it in daily life. We are tempted to focus more on the achievements, relationships, goals, status, and possessions we want that we do not have. We are largely concerned with what we think we deserve. Because of this, the gratitude most people know and practice is a distorted, lesser version, marked primarily by sentimentalism or routine. But sentimentalism and routine are not at all what God's Word encourages or commands.

Saying "thank you" can certainly be an expression of the kind of gratitude God commands. So can gathering with family and friends each year to celebrate the reasons you have to give thanks. If you sing songs of praise to God every Sunday at church, that can be an expression of gratitude, too. But those practices, in and of themselves, are not what God is after. True gratitude isn't merely an event. Neither is it just an expression of affection or nostalgia. For people who were dead in sin and are now alive in Christ, gratitude should be a continual condition of the heart that shows up practically in everyday life.

That's why Paul prayed for the believers in Colossae to keep on being grateful, to grow in gratitude (Col 1:9-14). His prayer is meant to inform our understanding and practice of true gratitude today, too. God isn't calling us to a routine of sentimentality at Thanksgiving and on Sundays. He wants us to be filled with gratitude every moment of every day, no matter what is going on in our lives. God has rescued us from darkness and brought us into Christ's eternal kingdom (v. 13). We have redemption. Our sins are forgiven (v. 14). What an amazing gift; what an amazing God!

This knowledge of God and experience of relationship with Him changes things. Yes, He is Creator, and it is right to be grateful for the people He has put in our lives. It is good to be thankful for turkey and dressing and sweet potato casserole—and jobs and houses and every single good thing we have because every single good thing we have is every bit the provision of God. Yet He calls us to a deeper understanding. True gratitude does not simply acknowledge what earthly blessings we have; it acknowledges God's ultimate, eternal work which remains true in every circumstance. Even in those things we want but do not have, God is our Redeemer. And redemption is transformational; it compels a life of gratitude that seeks to "walk worthy of the Lord, fully pleasing to Him: bearing fruit in every good work and growing in the knowledge of God" (v. 10).

So what does that look like? How do we practice biblical gratitude beyond writing thank you notes and listening to worship music as we drive to the store to buy this year's pumpkin pie? How do we show that we are genuinely grateful for the salvation we have been given in Jesus Christ? What was Paul praying for the Colossians to do? What was he, in effect, praying for you to do?

Acknowledge God's work of salvation in Jesus Christ—*to God Himself.*

There is no other starting point for practicing biblical gratitude. This is not sentimental acknowledgement, driven solely by emotion or routine acknowledgement, driven solely by tradition, ritual, or expectation. Instead, this is an acknowledgement of truth and grace, where the understanding of personal sin meets the gift of Christ's blood sacrifice on the cross and chooses to follow Him in faith.

Have you acknowledged God's work of salvation in Jesus Christ in this way? If not, you can take that step right now! Use the space on the next page to tell your story to God, in light of His story (or simply speak it to Him out loud). Confess that you are dead in sin and in need of His Son Jesus to give you life. Recognize that it is by His grace through faith alone in Jesus—not any good works you do—that you can be saved.

Acknowledge that Jesus is Lord and that He died on the cross and rose from the dead to redeem your life. Gratefully profess your decision to turn from your sin and follow Him.

If today is your first time to acknowledge God's work of salvation in Jesus Christ in this way, use the space to tell your story to God again, in light of His story, as a way of practicing a lifestyle of gratitude.

MY STORY IN LIGHT OF GOD'S STORY

Then they cried out to the LORD in their trouble; he rescued them from their distress.

PSALM 107:6

Acknowledge God's work of salvation in Jesus Christ and share it with another person.

Our whole lives are to be lived as a demonstration of gratitude to God for what He has done. And whole-life gratitude acknowledges God's work everywhere—at home, at work, at church, in your neighborhood, in your community, and even around the world.

If you're already a Christian, use the space below to write your faith story (your testimony) in three to five sentences. Then practice sharing it with another person so that you will be more ready to acknowledge God's work of salvation in Jesus Christ as opportunities arise in the days ahead.

MY FAITH STORY

THANKS BE TO GOD FOR HIS *indescribable* GIFT!

2 Corinthians 9:15

REFLECTION

As you finish your week of study, take a moment to process what you've learned and how your heart has been stirred concerning gratitude. Use the space below however you wish—write a prayer of thanks to the Lord, summarize what you've learned, write a poem, create a list of what you're grateful for, draw a picture, write a song, confess your struggle to be grateful, or document other expressions of your heart.

FOR THE GROUP TIME

If you're doing this study with a group, consider the following questions and be ready to discuss during your time together. (If you're leading the group, check out the leader guide at lifeway.com/grateful to help you prepare.)

Which day was your favorite day of study? Why?

What stood out to you from this week of personal study? What has stuck with you? What surprised you or was new information?

What's one thing you learned this week that will help you cultivate a heart of gratitude? How will you apply what you learned?

To continue developing and nurturing a heart of gratitude, get a copy of the *Gratitude Prayer Journal* at lifeway.com/grateful.

WEEK TWO

GRATEFUL FOR GOD'S PRESENCE

Now that we have a foundational understanding of what we have to be thankful for in Jesus, this week we'll consider why gratitude is an important, everyday part of how we live for Him.

How does an awareness of God's presence with us in the day-to-day change our perspective? What does it look like for us to worship God through thanksgiving, like David did? Or when Paul tells us to "give thanks in everything," what did he really mean, and how do we do that? Let's see what we can discover together.

Meaningful MOMENTS

by Emily Wickham

God's presence holds countless delights: the warmth of His welcome, the satisfaction of His love, and so much more. While the Lord draws near whenever and wherever I pursue Him, I especially enjoy reading the Bible and praying in nature's midst, connecting with the Living One while appreciating His handiwork. The God of the universe—the Savior of the world—desires relationship with you and me. Isn't that incredible? And I'm so grateful. Time spent in His presence results in meaningful moments that fill us with praise.

The Old Testament experience of God's presence, however, differs from our current interactions. While "we have boldness to enter the sanctuary through the blood of Jesus" (Heb. 10:19), saints before Christ didn't possess this freedom. They didn't have personal relationships with God like we enjoy. They were represented before God by priests, more specifically, the high priest. Once a year, on the Day of Atonement, the high priest would enter into the most holy place, an inner chamber of the tabernacle (later the temple) to present a sacrifice for his sin and the sin of the people (Lev. 16). He was to take blood from the sacrifice and sprinkle it against the mercy seat of the ark of the covenant. The ark represented God's throne[1] where His "presence hovered above the seat, between the cherubim, when He talked to the priest."[2] But what was the ark, and where did it originate?

> READ EXODUS 25:10-22. List the details you learn about the ark from this passage.

The ark was crafted from acacia wood and overlaid inside and out with gold. The Ten Commandments—"stone tablets inscribed by the finger of God" (Ex. 31:18)—were contained within, and the golden mercy seat, an exquisite piece that included one cherub on each end, covered the ark. As stated, once per year, Israel's high priest offered sacrificial blood on this mercy seat for his and the people's sins (Heb. 9:7), picturing a future day when Christ's precious blood would be shed on the cross for our sins. The ark of God also held significance because the Lord designated it as the place He'd communicate with Moses (Ex. 25:22).

During the time of the judges, the ark was captured by the Philistines. They only kept it a short time because "the LORD's hand was against" them while the ark was in their possession (1 Sam. 5:6,9). They sent it back to Israel, and after a couple of fateful incidents (1 Sam. 6; 2 Sam. 6), it finally ended up at the house of Obed-Edom.

READ 1 CHRONICLES 15.

Cymbals, harps, and lyres resounded with melody, accompanied by shouts, horns, and trumpets. Singers lifted their voices in exaltation, and joy radiated from people's faces. King David had arranged this magnificent procession with careful attention to God's commands, which resulted in the Lord's help with their journey. The Levites sacrificed bulls and rams in response as they properly carried the ark of God to Jerusalem.

As alluded to earlier, David's first attempt to bring the ark to Jerusalem resulted in Uzzah's death. The king had failed to follow God's instructions for relocating the holy vessel, but this time he and the people obeyed.

> According to 1 Chronicles 15:13, why didn't the Israelites know how to transfer the ark the first time they tried to move it to Jerusalem?

Sin carries consequences. Although we're "not under the law but under grace" (Rom. 6:14), God values obedience "from the heart" (Rom. 6:17). Like the Israelites, let's learn from past mistakes.

You might wonder why the ark matters to us today since Christians don't even worship in the tabernacle or temple. But there's something beautiful for us to see in this story of moving the ark.

David longed for God's presence. Though imperfect, he repeatedly sought God. And since the ark hosted God's presence, the king labored to place it in Israel's capital city. The ark brought God near.

Today, *Christ* is the way to the Father. When Jesus died on the cross, the temple veil was torn from top to bottom, indicating God's acceptance of Christ's perfect sacrifice for our sins. Hallelujah! Nothing blocks us from God's presence. But sometimes we allow busyness, selfishness, distractions, and more to prevent us from interacting with God.

Like David, let's yearn for God's presence. Let's daily seek His face, for James 4:8 reads, "Draw near to God, and he will draw near to you."

How does King David's journey in moving the ark encourage you to pursue God?

READ 1 CHRONICLES 16:1-26.

The Levites triumphantly placed the ark in its tent. David had navigated the pressures in bringing it to Jerusalem, and relief rippled through his spirit. Because he'd learned more about God in the process, he couldn't contain his elation. Gratitude for God's presence overflowed like a waterfall.

Describe a situation in which you're trying to follow God. What is He teaching you about Himself along the way?

As the king launched his psalm of thanksgiving, he urged the people to give thanks and seek God's face. He also guided the people to remember. David knew recalling God's mighty acts would lead the Israelites to deeper admiration for their Creator, the one true God.

Based on verses 12-22, what did God do for the Israelites?

In verse 24, David emphasized telling the nations of God's glory. His greatness prevails; He alone is God. Just as Israel's existence and progress testified of God and His power, the Lord's work in us proclaims Him. Let's openly exalt God like David. Our testimony can strengthen fellow Christians and lead others to faith.

Journal about something wonderful the Lord has done for you. Who will you share this testimony with this week?

READ 1 CHRONICLES 16:27-43.

The king understood a wealth of magnificence surrounds the Lord, so he exhorted all to worship Him "in the splendor of his holiness" (1 Chron. 16:29). God's attributes inspire worship filled with reverence and honor.

Which of God's qualities in verses 27-36 captivate you, and why?

David further noted nature's delight in God: the heavens are glad, the earth rejoices, the seas resound, the fields exult, and the trees shout. Lastly, he uttered thanks, expressing a complete circle of gratitude from beginning to end. "Give thanks to the LORD, for he is good; his faithful love endures forever" (1 Chron. 16:34).

David's successful delivery of the ark to Jerusalem enhanced his gratitude for God, and it also motivated him to entrust the ark's daily care and protection to qualified men. The king's thankful heart affected every aspect of worshiping God.

Let's never lose sight of God's splendor, showing reverence as we "seek the LORD and his strength; seek his face always" (1 Chron. 16:11). At the same time, let's pursue the intimacy He offers. Despite God's holy magnificence, He stoops to relate with humble people. *Wow—we can connect with the Majesty on High.*

Worship the Lord with gratitude by writing your own prayer of thanksgiving below.

Thankful HEARTS

by Erin Franklin

When my younger cousin, Grace, was around four years old, she and her family were saying their goodbyes to the rest of the extended family after finishing Thanksgiving dinner. One of the familial hosts wanted them to take home leftovers, so she asked if she could pack up some green beans, sweet potatoes, and an array of other vegetables and sides for them.

"I'll take that turkey," my cousin responded without missing a beat. (You need to understand that during the family dinner, everyone had eaten one turkey. So what my cousin was requesting to take home was not exactly "leftovers" but rather a second uneaten, *whole* turkey.) Graciously, the host gave it to her. So little Grace walked out the door with a whole turkey in a bowl bigger than she was.

When my family retells this story, we laugh at the forthrightness of my cousin's request that resulted in such a bountiful gift. But as my cousin (who is now in her twenties) and I were recently recounting this story, she said she's also so thankful for the family member who was willing to give her such a generous gift despite her childish request. Although she enjoyed the temporary gift of the turkey, looking back now, she is much more grateful for the gracious giver's presence in her life.

Gratitude needs to be an everyday part of the Christian life, and intentionally worshiping God with thanksgiving in our hearts and remembering the blessings He has given us helps us develop an attitude of thankfulness. Often in prayer, we use this direct communication with God to simply check off all our requests—good health, guidance, forgiveness, and so forth—without remembering to thank the Giver for His presence in our lives and the blessings He gives us. Scripture clearly tells us it is good for us to present our requests to God, but we are to do so with *thanksgiving.* (See Phil. 4:6; Col. 1:3.) Praying and worshiping with thanksgiving protects our hearts from developing a demanding and grumbling spirit.

> **READ PHILIPPIANS 4:6-7.** What does it look like to present requests to God with thanksgiving in your prayers?

List a few of your current prayer requests in the left column of the chart below. Then, in the right column, write how you can specifically show thankfulness as you pray that request.

PRAYERS & PETITIONS	WITH THANKSGIVING

God doesn't always answer our requests in the ways we desire, but when we communicate with a thankful heart, He will give us peace that passes all understanding to humbly accept His will. Philippians is considered one of the prison epistles, traditionally dated as written during Paul's first Roman imprisonment. Paul also wrote Colossians during this time.

READ COLOSSIANS 3:12-17. What are some of the godly characteristics a believer should display?

In the verses right before this section, Paul told the Colossians to put to death the sinful characteristics of the old man—sexual immorality, impurity, lust, and so forth. He also told them to put off things like malice, anger, slander, and lying. Then in verses 12-17, he instructed the believers to "put on" virtues indicative of Christian living—such as compassion, kindness, and humility. These virtues aren't practiced in a vacuum. They are tested in our relationships.[3]

For example, look up the definition of compassion, and write it here.

Compassion is:

Merriam-Webster defines compassion as "sympathetic consciousness of others' distress together with a desire to alleviate it."[4] Therefore, in order to show compassion, we must see others, recognize they are hurting, and desire to help them. Similar to how these virtues are exhibited through interaction with others, Paul encouraged the Colossians to be thankful *together*, emphasizing this command in verses 15, 16, and 17.

REREAD VERSES 15-17. How is gratitude one of the ways we worship God?

Practically, what are some ways you can practice communal thanksgiving and worship?

In verses 16-17, Paul instructed them to give thanks as they taught and encouraged one another through singing to God. This passage helps us see that a grateful heart and the act of thanksgiving undergird our worship. He understood that thankful hearts are those that are ready and able to fully rejoice in the peace of Christ and praise of God.

The theme of thankfulness runs throughout the letter to the Colossians. Despite his clearly difficult circumstances of imprisonment, Paul began the letter with gratitude.

LOOK BACK TO COLOSSIANS 1 AND READ VERSES 1-8.
What was Paul thankful for and why?

Before he instructed the readers of this letter to practice gratitude in 3:12-17, Paul showed what a thankful heart looks like. Sometimes it feels difficult to rejoice and be grateful in our everyday walk with Christ when life's current circumstances feel unbearable. Just because Paul said he was grateful and joyful doesn't mean he was simply putting on a happy exterior that somehow allowed him to ignore all human feelings of suffering. In 2 Corinthians 11:16-33, Paul didn't shy away from listing several horrible things he endured—beatings, a multitude of dangers, hunger, and coldness, just to name a few. On top of the physical hardship he endured, he said he faced "*daily* pressure" with his concern for all the churches (v. 28, emphasis added). Yet throughout his epistles, Paul always expressed an attitude of thankfulness and exhorted his readers to do the same.

REREAD VERSES 4-5 IN COLOSSIANS 1. Do you notice a familiar triad in these verses? What is it? Turn to 1 Corinthians 13:13 to help you with your answer.

Paul believed this trio of faith, hope, and love was eternally united, and this message shows up again and again in his teaching. (See Rom. 5:1-5; Gal. 5:5-6; 1 Thess. 1:3; 5:8.) Paul was thankful for the Colossians' *faith* in Christ and *love* for all the saints—both known because of their *hope* in eternity. As this triad figured prominently in Paul's view of good Christian character and conduct, he was thankful the believers understood the value of these great Christian virtues as well.

Following Paul's example, how can you daily cultivate a virtuous heart of gratitude even on the hard days?

No one in this broken world is spared from suffering and trials, but as believers, we can worship God with thanksgiving because of the foundational hope we have of an eternity free from sin and heartache (Rev. 21:4). Being grateful doesn't mean forgoing lament. Being grateful means upholding a humble consciousness of the relational faith, eternally significant hope, and unifying love we find through God's presence every day.

MY Strength AND MY SONG

by Irene Sun

Every person comes to Jesus because of a desire. Blind people want to see. Lame people want to walk. I came to Jesus because I wanted a friend.

I was fourteen, and I was bullied at school every day. I remember singing "As the Deer" before leaving the house every morning. It was the first song I learned to play on the piano that my teacher did not assign. The lyrics that speak of God being my friend and brother and how He is my strength and shield brought me comfort and peace.

In God's sovereignty, the Holy Spirit made me a new person that year. In my longing to belong, Love found me. Jesus sat by me in the classroom. He walked with me in the hallways. He even protected me and defended me against bullies. He was my one true and never-failing Friend.

Psalm 118 gives thanks to God for His presence. He is with us. We are not alone.

READ PSALM 118.

The first and last lines establish the foundation of this psalm: "Give thanks to Yahweh, for he is good. His faithful love endures forever." This literary device is called an *inclusio*—bookends.

What does it mean that God is good? Is He good like dark chocolate? Is He good like dogs when they obey their owners' commands? Is it because He gives us the desires of our hearts?

What do we mean when we say "God is good"?

In Exodus 33:19, Yahweh promised Moses that He would cause His goodness to pass before Moses. His goodness encapsulates His mercy, compassion, forgiveness, faithfulness, grace, and His steadfast love, His *hesed*—which was mentioned not once but twice when the Lord actually passed before Moses (Ex. 34:6-7).

Yahweh is good because He forgives our sins and offenses. He is holy. His presence is like the sun, exposing all that is hidden in the darkness. He knows we are not good. He does not turn a blind eye to sin. His presence is not a "judgment free zone." There is judgment in His presence, but there is also compassion and mercy.

His presence is holy, but there is also forgiveness and acceptance. This is true goodness, deep goodness, goodness that draws us into His presence.

> Notice where the name Yahweh occurs in Psalm 118. (In our English Bibles, the name *Yahweh* is represented by the word L ORD [in small caps].)

> What are the different ways Yahweh makes Himself known?

VERSES 1-12

Yahweh is everywhere. His name is repeated over and over again in this psalm. Repetition is a foundational method of learning. Repetition slows us down and presses the words into our souls.

Hebrew poetry is written in parallel lines, which is the art of repeating an idea with variation, in different ways. Parallel lines complete an idea, deepen understanding, and draw contrasts. Here are some examples from this text.

A // A′

Some parallel lines are synonymous. Together, they make a complete thought. Verses 6 and 7 are synonymous, "The L ORD is for me" and "The L ORD is my helper."

A // B // C

Some parallel lines add new ideas to the first line, like a staircase. Together, they deepen our understanding and move us forward. Verses 2, 3, and 4, deepen an idea. By repeating the phrase "His faithful love endures forever," notice how the circle of those who praise Yahweh gets smaller.

Israel > house of Aaron > those who fear Yahweh

A // Z

Some parallel lines are antithetical to the one before. Together, the contrasting lines clarify and compare the ideas to help us understand. Verses 8 and 9 draw contrasts between trusting Yahweh and trusting human power.

VERSES 13-18

Verses 13 to 18 create a more complex form of multiple parallel lines.

A
    B
        C
            D
        C'
    B'
A'

This pattern is called a *chiastic structure*. A *chiasm* is a literary device that uses parallel lines in order to frame what is in the center.

> Notice the parallel lines (A // A', B // B', C // C') and what is in the center of this chiasm (D). (Note: this is my personal translation of the Hebrew text.)

A	¹³ Pushing, you pushed me to fall, and Yahweh helped me
B	¹⁴ Yahweh is my strength, my song, my salvation
C	¹⁵ Shouts of joys and victory in the tents of the righteous
D	The right hand of Yahweh acts valiantly
C'	¹⁶ The right hand of Yahweh is raised and acts valiantly
B'	¹⁷ I will not die but live and proclaim what Yahweh has done
A'	¹⁸ Disciplining, Yahweh disciplined me, but to Death he did not give me

"Pushing, you push me to fall." Who is pushing us? Is it our enemies that were like bees and fire among thorns (vv. 10-12)? Perhaps. But look, verse 13 parallels verse 18. In verse 18, "Disciplining, Yahweh disciplined me" exactly parallel the verb tenses of verse 13. What if the One who disciplines us is also the one who pushes us?

The ambiguity of who is doing the pushing is purposeful because the answer may be both: God and our enemies. Throughout Scripture, God disciplines His people through their enemies.

Think of some examples of God disciplining His people in Scripture: when God sent Adam and Eve out of the garden, when David's census caused a national plague, when Israel fell to Assyria, when Judah fell to Babylon, when God sent Israel into exile. The consequences of sin resulted in immeasurable losses and immense pain. But these momentary disciplines were given to move us back toward Yahweh, to keep us from being separated from Him forever.

Yahweh's presence is sometimes perceived and known in our pain. In Psalm 23, David is not afraid, even when he finds himself in the valley of the shadow of death because Yahweh is with him. How does he know he is not alone? The shepherd's rod and staff comfort him.

We give thanks for Yahweh's presence. Yahweh's presence is communicated to us in His blessings. But as the songwriter Laura Story tells us in her song "Blessings," sometimes blessings come through raindrops and tears, through difficulties and trials.[5]

What is hard about your day and your season right now?

God's discipline is a blessing because it reveals His steadfast love (*hesed*) (vv. 1-4). *Hesed* is God's life-giving, unchanging, saving love. *Hesed* is a merciful act to save someone's life. He gives us pain and crushes our pride not for our harm but for our salvation. He saves us to be with Him. He desires to give us Himself and to make us holy. His correction reassures us that we belong to Him. We are His, and we are not alone.

Notice the center of the chiastic structure in verses 13-18, "The right hand of Yahweh acts valiantly." The right hand of Yahweh that does valor is a nail-pierced hand. In the throes of God's discipline, we forget the wound on the Shepherd's hand. He is good, and He forgives. When we were sinners, the Shepherd "bore our sins in his body on the tree . . . By his wounds you have been healed" (1 Pet. 2:24). Behold, this is love.

GIVE *Thanks* IN EVERYTHING

by Tessa Morrell

To begin today's study, let's be honest. Trusting God and giving thanks in everything is sometimes difficult. It's absolutely possible and completely worth it, but sometimes it requires great intentionality and fierce determination. It requires a surrendered heart and confidence in the God in whom we trust.

What we'll study today is not an easy aspect of faith, but it's one that fosters rich communion with God and others, and ultimately, as we will see near the end of the passage, God will do the work in our hearts because He is faithful. Let's dive in and discover His word for us today.

The final section of Paul's first letter to the Thessalonians is a collection of exhortations. It's filled with brief statements of direction and encouragement related to several aspects of the Christian life.

READ 1 THESSALONIANS 5:12-15.

Paul begins this section of the letter by instructing his brothers and sisters in Thessalonica to recognize and honor those who lead them in the Lord. In other places in Scripture, it's clear that those with a position of influence and leadership in the church have a great responsibility to lead in a way that honors the Lord (Titus 2:7-8; Jas. 3:1). They are accountable for their teaching, how they lead, and the way they live.

What are some reasons a person in leadership in the church might need encouragement and recognition?

What are some ways you can honor the leaders in your church?

Who is a leader whose influence has made a difference in your life spiritually?

Consider writing that person a note of encouragement, thanking him or her for loving the Lord and you with great faithfulness.

If your story includes pain connected to a leader or leaders in the church, pray for the Lord to bring an example into your life of healthy, God-honoring leadership. Grieve what you have experienced, and continue trusting that God will heal your heart and restore your faith in Him and in those He's chosen to lead His church.

In verses 14-15, Paul gave several brief instructions related to relationships with other people. List them below.

How would following these instructions strengthen a family of believers? What benefits would these actions have in relationships?

Paul challenged the church to minister to those who were struggling—the idle, the discouraged, and the weak. But then he broadened his instructions by encouraging the church to bear with everyone, regardless of what was going on in their lives. And to seek what was good in all their relationships. Paul knew the church was made up of people prone to sin. His instructions were to help hold the body of Christ together.

Paul continued his rapid-fire instructions to the church by listing a few more brief exhortations, including the command in verse 16 to "rejoice always."

TURN TO PHILIPPIANS 4:4 and write it out in the space below.

What do you think it means to "rejoice always," and why is that an instruction for God's people?

Next, in 1 Thessalonians 5:17, Paul says to "pray constantly."

Practically speaking, what are some ways you can "pray constantly"?

The concept of rejoicing always and praying constantly flows naturally into the instruction to "give thanks in everything." One of the reasons we rejoice always and pray throughout the day is to keep our minds fixed on the Lord. And it's from that connection with Him that our hearts will overflow with gratitude for who He is and what He has done and is doing in our lives.

It's important to recognize that while verse 18 fits perfectly in a study about gratitude, it's set within a context that describes several spiritual disciplines. Gratitude is not something that happens in isolation, apart from the other ways we grow in Christ. It's interconnected with the other aspects of transformation God does in our hearts as we follow Him.

One of the other relevant aspects concerning the context of this verse is the fact that Paul was writing to a group of people who understood difficult circumstances.

In 1 Thessalonians 1:6, Paul commended them for welcoming the message of the gospel despite "severe persecution." And in 2:14, he spoke of the sufferings they had experienced from their own people. Then Paul explained in 1 Thessalonians 3 that he had sent Timothy to Thessalonica to strengthen and encourage them "so that no one will be shaken by these afflictions" (3:3). When Timothy arrived, he was encouraged to discover the church was being faithful to the Lord and standing firm in their faith, despite their difficulties.

Paul didn't instruct them to "give thanks in everything" because their lives were easy. He instructed them to give thanks in everything, knowing it was difficult.

Gratitude is a worthwhile daily pursuit. It's all about consistency. We give thanks to the Lord even when life is hard. Honestly, it's most important to cultivate a thankful heart especially when life is hard.

> What is a current circumstance or area of your life that you would consider an "affliction"? How can you cultivate a heart of thanksgiving in the midst of that situation?

In the next four verses, Paul gives additional direction for spiritual growth. He wanted the Thessalonians to cling to what is true—what comes directly from the Lord through His Spirit and the words of His people. To "hold on to what is good" is an active choice to focus on what is true and good and honoring to the Lord.

READ 1 THESSALONIANS 5:23-24.

Finally, as Paul closed his letter, he transitioned into a blessing and hopeful prayer for the Thessalonians.

> What is God's role in the sanctification process? What is your role?

I think one of the most encouraging verses in this passage is verse 24. It reminds us that God is faithful. He calls us, and He will do the work in our hearts to transform us to look more like Jesus. There is no doubt. He will do it. His faithfulness is rooted in His character, therefore He can never fail.

How does knowing God is faithful provide you with peace and confidence in Him and His work in your life?

First Thessalonians 5:12-24 is filled to the brim with meaningful instruction not only for the church Paul was writing to, but for us today.

What is one action from verses 13-15 you can implement into your relationships this week?

Write a prayer of thanksgiving to God that's directly related to a difficult situation in your life. Be honest with Him, and thank Him for an aspect of His character that you are especially grateful for in this season.

Gratitude LEADS TO INTIMACY

by Cynthia Hopkins

like to think I'm a positive person—I see the bright side of things, my glass tends to be half-full, and all that. When I was growing up, that particular personality trait annoyed my two brothers. From time to time, we got in trouble for fighting with each other and were sent to our rooms. Within minutes, though, I typically let go of whatever had us completely enraged, knocked on the wall my younger brother and I shared, grabbed a tennis ball, opened my door, sat down, and invited him to play a game of catch, doorway to doorway. He usually agreed but with a scowl that lasted for most of the game.

Still today, I try to let things go quickly and focus on reasons to be grateful. I know those reasons are innumerable in Christ. The trouble is, life has gotten a lot tougher than childish disagreements with my siblings. Rolling a tennis ball back and forth no longer has the power to repair the damage that people and difficult circumstances cause. So, although I have many reasons to be grateful, my mind often takes off in an alternate direction. My guess is that you will agree—when life gives us lemons, our first inclination isn't usually to make lemonade. It's to squirt those lemons in someone's eyes!

That's one reason I love the psalms. In them, we find God's people singing songs of grateful praise, even when life was hard. This is not to say they were always optimistic or chose the kind path. King David candidly acknowledged his desire for God to do far worse to his enemies than squirting them with lemons. At the same time, though, David rested in God's presence and was *grateful*.

> IN PSALM 63, we find both realities in one circumstance. Take a minute now to read it.

David was on the run in the wilderness, most likely from his son Absalom who intended to kill him. It was one of the most difficult seasons of David's life. But in that season, David honestly grieved *and* gratefully praised God. As David related to God in those seemingly dichotomous ways, his relationship with God grew more intimate. Physically and emotionally, David was dry and desolate. But because God was with him, he found that he could be spiritually satisfied.

I've never been on the run from literal enemies in the wilderness, but I can relate to David in a more figurative sense. On the heels of the pandemic and just two weeks after moving to a new city, I was diagnosed with two brain aneurysms, both in danger of rupture. That discovery was noticeably providential, and I was certainly grateful to God. At the same time, it made for a wilderness-type experience. I was in a new city in a new church trying to make new friends. And over the course of the year, I had four different procedures to deal with the aneurysms—the last of which was major brain surgery with a long period of recovery.

Because the pandemic had surgeries backed up a full six weeks, that's how long I had to wait for my procedure. It didn't take a huge amount of discernment for me to recognize that, over those weeks, there would be times when my thoughts would take off down a wrong path—likely around two or three in the morning. I didn't want to let distorted, fearful thoughts roam freely in my mind, but I knew that in a wilderness season, those can easily enter and exist alone, wholly separate from gratitude.

I needed God's presence like never before in those weeks of waiting. I also knew I would need God's presence the day of my surgery and in the days and weeks to follow. So I chose one verse from each of the sixty-six books of the Bible, typed them in a document, and then memorized them. Some I knew; most I learned. And when those wrong thoughts came, and they *did*, I was ready. God's Word made me ready. Each time I had a moment of fear and uncertainty, my thoughts turned to Genesis and then started recalling verses through Revelation that reminded me God was with me. Fear and uncertainty turned to gratitude.

Would God have been with me even if I hadn't memorized Scripture? Would God have been with David even if he hadn't meditated on Scripture through the night? Of course! God isn't with us because we memorize Scripture. God is with us because that's who God is. What Scripture memorization and meditation do is help us recognize and acknowledge God's presence when our circumstances tempt us to think we are all alone.

Gratitude necessitates a change in perspective, and that takes intentionality. So read God's Word. Meditate on it. Memorize it. God's presence is always with you, but you must spend time with Him to realize it and respond in gratitude when difficult seasons come.

No one is asking you to tackle sixty-six verses this week (unless you just really want to!) But would you commit to memorizing a few? Scripture memory is a spiritual discipline God will use to help you practice gratitude as He points you to the reality of His presence. Paul expressed it like this in 2 Corinthians 10:4b-5: *We demolish arguments and every proud thing that is raised up against the knowledge of God, and we take every thought captive to obey Christ.*

So how do you take every thought captive? Confront them with the knowledge of who God is, what He does, and what He promises to do! Look up the verses below, and record them in the space provided. Then choose three to five to memorize.

Numbers 23:19

Job 19:25-27

Joel 2:13

Nahum 1:7

John 16:33

Ephesians 3:20-21

Jude 1:25

GIVE THANKS TO THE LORD *for He is good;* HIS FAITHFUL LOVE ENDURES FOREVER.

Psalm 107:1

REFLECTION

As you finish your week of study, take a moment to process what you've learned and how your heart has been stirred concerning gratitude. Use the space below however you wish—write a prayer of thanks to the Lord, summarize what you've learned, write a poem, create a list of what you're grateful for, draw a picture, write a song, confess your struggle to be grateful, or document other expressions of your heart.

FOR THE GROUP TIME

If you're doing this study with a group, consider the following questions and be ready to discuss during your time together. (If you're leading the group, check out the leader guide at lifeway.com/grateful to help you prepare.)

Which day was your favorite day of study? Why?

What stood out to you from this week of personal study? What has stuck with you? What surprised you or was new information?

What's one thing you learned this week that will help you cultivate a heart of gratitude? How will you apply what you learned?

To continue developing and nurturing a heart of gratitude, get a copy of the *Gratitude Prayer Journal* at lifeway.com/grateful.

WEEK THREE

GRATEFUL FOR GOD'S WORK IN AND THROUGH US

To begin this week of study, we'll look at the story of the Philippian jailer in Acts 16. In a moment of fear, the jailer asked Paul and Silas "What must I do to be saved?" Through the jailer's joyful and generous response to the gospel as well as the teachings of Jesus and Paul, we're reminded that gratefulness is a key characteristic in the life of a believer. A grateful heart also has huge implications for the way we love others.

GIVING *Thanks* TO GOD IN THE HARD TIMES

by Janice Gaines

Across the nation and world, we hear conversations from different sides about what is owed to them and what is rightfully theirs. But this is not a conversation just other people are having; I participate also. But what if we all responded to life—even life that has been shifted or shattered by circumstances outside of our control—with gratitude? What might that gratitude yield in our lives and the lives of others that encounter our gratitude? Acts 16:16-34 tells us the story of the Philippian jailer and how gratitude radically changed the outcome.

READ ACTS 16:16-24.

Paul and Silas had been traveling and sharing the gospel in Macedonia prompted by a vision Paul had of a Macedonian man asking them to come and help them. In obedience to God, they traveled to that area and stayed for some days in Philippi, one of the leading cities of the district. According to the verses immediately preceding this passage, they were already seeing fruit from sharing the gospel.

Then, one day they encountered a slave girl with a spirit of divination who followed them around crying out about who they were and what they were doing. The Scripture says she did this for many days. She was actually telling the truth, but the problem seems to have been how she was telling it. This declaring of their mission through the streets without context was most likely not the way Paul wanted to introduce the gospel or his personal mission to the people of Philippi.[1] Annoyed, Paul commanded the spirit to come out of her. As a result, her divination powers ceased and her owners were upset that they could no longer make a profit from her.

The angry owners confronted Paul and Silas and dragged them in front of the chief magistrates, who were responsible for maintaining civil order for the Roman government. The owners' accusations were more instigation than truth, seemingly to rile up anyone listening to get the results they desired. As the gathered crowd joined in the accusations, the chief magistrates stripped Paul and Silas and ordered them to be beaten. After the beating, the magistrates ordered them to be put into prison and guarded closely. Upon hearing this order, the jailer put them in the inner prison and fastened their feet in stocks. We can ascertain that the jailer took his job seriously.

What would you do if you were beaten severely, wrongly imprisoned (by both moral and legal standards), tossed into the deepest, darkest cell, and chained to the wall? I would probably have to fight frustration, anger, and feelings of injustice. And I would have eagerly prepared to plead my case since Roman law would have said that I had one. (It was illegal in Roman law to beat with a rod or imprison a Roman citizen without giving them a trial first.)[2] Paul and Silas, though, committed the night to prayer and singing hymns.

Take a second to put yourself in Paul and Silas's shoes. When was the last time you felt mistreated? How did you respond?

What differences do you see in Paul and Silas's responses and your own?

What helps you respond with grace to being treated unfairly? How does being a follower of Christ affect your response?

The right perspective is key to a Christ-honoring response in the face of injustice. If you're mistreated because of your faith, as Paul and Silas were, remembering the reason you're suffering can give you the strength to act with grace. Plus, taking the long view helps with the right response. Looking ahead to a time and place without suffering can help you look beyond mistreatment.

READ ACTS 16:25-27.

Around midnight, as the jailer was sleeping and Paul and Silas were worshiping, a powerful earthquake shook the prison! The doors were opened and the prisoners' chains loosencd. This alarmed the jailer a great deal. He was personally responsible for the prisoners, so he would be held accountable for their escape, possibly facing the lethal fate intended for those on his watch. (See Acts 12:18-19.)[3]

> Once again, put yourself in Paul and Silas's position. What might you do if the person responsible for harming you was about to "get what was coming to them" after a miraculous intervention by God Himself? Would you see God's action as His divine punishment on the one who hurt you? Or would you get away from the situation as fast as possible? Or maybe ask God why He intervened and what you should do next? Explain.

Let's read on to see what Paul and Silas did.

READ ACTS 16:28-34.

The response of Paul and Silas was not normal. Instead of choosing freedom, they stayed in the jail, as did all the other prisoners. When Paul announced this to the jailer, the jailer immediately rushed into the prison, fell at Paul and Silas's feet, and asked, "What must I do to be saved?" It's interesting that he had language for something he did not yet know how to access. What did he mean by those words? He wasn't pleading for his physical safety. That was not in question since the prisoners were still there. Instead that language most likely came from hearing Paul and Silas's testimony in prayers and songs about God's saving power. How else would he have known how to concisely sum up what he needed from them? The jailer responded to what God had been speaking in his hearing for the last little while.

> What has God been repeating in your hearing recently? How can you respond in obedience to what He's calling you to?

Paul and Silas's faith and Christ-focused perspective prompted their response of grateful worship in the midst of their horrible circumstances. Their response also affected those around them. Their fellow prisoners didn't rush to escape, and the Philippian jailer pursued the very salvation Paul and Silas were praying and singing about. The effect didn't stop there. Not only did salvation come to the jailer but also to his household. Then out of new found joy and certain gratefulness, the jailer physically cared for Paul and Silas, washing their wounds and showing them hospitality. He went from being a diligent jailer to a grateful believer.

This passage shows how our gratitude for how God has worked in and through us is a testimony to those around us that often produces gratitude in them. Their expressed gratitude can then result in gratitude in others, and the cycle goes on and on.

> How will you respond today to the circumstances outside of your control? In what ways can you express gratitude to God that will affect those around you?

CULTIVATING *Gratitude* IN COMMUNITY

by Ravin McKelvy

I n recent years, *community* seems to be a buzz word in our culture. In an increasingly media-connected world, feeling disconnected from genuine relationships appears to be on the incline. From Christ-followers to non-believers, many people are trying to find the key to a thriving community. My friends and I have often discussed this topic, trying to determine the problem. One of the most prevalent obstacles we've noticed is the pervasive feeling of jealousy or competition toward others because of what we see on social media. The constant lure to compare or covet is always before us. But I believe the answer to combating this is found in Philippians 1:3-11. This passage gives us an example of what it looks like to have true community in Christ—and it starts with gratitude.

> **READ PHILIPPIANS 1:3-11.** Is your heart filled with gratitude when you see the Lord's goodness in someone else's life, or do you find yourself struggling with jealousy? Explain.

CULTIVATE GRATITUDE BY REMEMBERING

In the Bible, we see God often calling His people to remembrance. Let's face it, we as humans are prone to forgetting. I can't recount the number of times I've forgotten where I've left my keys or what I walked into a room to look for or even my thoughts as I'm speaking. Those incidents are a small example of my forgetfulness. But I will admit, at times, I have also forgotten the goodness of God or His faithfulness in the midst of trials or to thank Him for the family He has brought me into through Christ.

Paul stated in this passage that he gave thanks every time he remembered the Philippians. Something I've started doing recently is keeping what I like to call a "book of delights." Whenever I have a good conversation with a friend or I learn more about the Lord from them, I quickly type a note about that experience into my notes app on my phone. At the end of the week, I go through all the notes and add them into a scrapbook. I've found that as I look back at all those moments from the week, I am filled with gratitude for the community that the Lord has provided for me. I am daily getting to witness the Lord's faithfulness in their lives and learn from the work He is doing in them. But I know it would be so easy to forget if I am not intentionally choosing remembrance. Cultivating gratitude requires us to remember—not only the Lord's faithfulness in our lives but also in the lives of our brothers and sisters in Christ.

How can you practice remembrance in your daily life as a way to cultivate gratitude?

Use the space below to write down a few memories of how the Lord's work in the lives of people around you has impacted your faith.

CULTIVATE GRATITUDE BY PRAYING

Something else Paul talked about in this passage was his prayer life for the church. Because we live in a world consumed with self-focus and self-growth, it's easy to let that also consume our prayers. But Paul joyfully and thankfully prayed for his brothers and sisters in Christ. He was grateful for their partnership in the gospel and trusted the Lord would complete His work in them. As we pray for our communities, we should be grateful for how God has put us together to accomplish His work and thank Him for how He is working in and through all of our lives.

Try setting an alarm on your phone for a specific time each week to pray for your community.

Write a prayer in the space below for your local church community and the church around the world.

CULTIVATE GRATITUDE BY CHERISHING

As Paul was writing this letter, he was in prison. He could have been storing fear or worry in his heart over his circumstances, but instead, he told the Philippians that he had them in his heart. He was able to cultivate gratitude by cherishing them and the work that the Lord was doing in their lives even when he was going through trials. And we are called to do the same.

This call is to a sort of radical counter-culturalism—one in which we love our brothers and sisters in Christ in such a way that we can rejoice in the work the Lord is doing in their lives, no matter the circumstances of our own lives.

To cherish our community is to be genuinely grateful for the work being done in their lives—knowing that we are all part of the same body. Yes, we are to weep with those who weep and rejoice with those who rejoice. But what a mystery and privilege it is to also be able to rejoice with others in our weeping or to weep with others in our rejoicing. I wonder if we would see a growth in gratitude in our lives if we truly cherished the work that God is doing in others as much as we did the work He is doing in us.

Another aspect of cherishing others is expressing your gratitude to them. In the entirety of the passage we read, Paul expressed to the Philippians his gratitude, not only for what the Lord was doing in and through them, but also for his relationship to them as their brother in Christ. Expressing our gratitude to each other is not just reserved for the "words of affirmation people." All of us are called to it. This will help us continue to cultivate a grateful heart.

> Send a message to a few people in your life, and tell them specific ways in which you are thankful for the Lord's work in their lives.

God is working in and through every member of His body on a personal level. And we bear a heart of gratitude in both the trials and triumphs, knowing that the Lord is carrying to completion the good work that He has started in each of us. I believe gratitude aids us in holding the tension of this individual yet communal reality. Being genuinely grateful for what the Lord is doing in others' lives can help combat jealousy in our trials and greed in our triumphs. Then we are better able to recognize the connection we have as siblings in Christ, fighting against disconnection. It is in our gratefulness that true, thriving community can take place.

> Spend a few minutes thanking the Lord for the work that you see Him doing in and through others' lives.

HIS *Name* AND HIS WORD

by Irene Sun

W e usually say "thank you" when we receive something we want. But worshipers of Yahweh give thanks even when we are given circumstances we do not want. Unbelievers give thanks for the good and desirable things they receive. The mark of a believer, however, is a thankful heart for all the gifts of God—in all the circumstances of life—some of which are undesirable and unexpected.

His name and His Word are unchanging, regardless of our present circumstances. Our best, most well-laid-out plan still falls so far short of God's wisdom. Gratitude for God's will means completely trusting His character (represented by His name) and His Word (that reveals His promises). Gratitude requires us to sacrifice our plans, desires, and purposes, and believe with all our hearts that He is for us and not against us. He is steadfast. He is faithful. He is good.

READ PSALM 138.

The superscription tells us who wrote this psalm. This is a psalm of David.

Who were the witnesses of David's singing (v. 1)?

The description of David's audience varies by translation:

NIV: before **THE "GODS"** I will sing your praise

ESV: before **THE GODS** I sing your praise

CSB: I will sing your praise before **THE HEAVENLY BEINGS**

These varying translations reveal a small conundrum. Why would David be singing before gods, "gods," or heavenly beings? Notice that he is not giving thanks to the gods. He is praising Yahweh in the presence of other gods.

The book of Psalm tells a story. Every psalm is part of the whole; one flows into the next. In order to understand Psalm 138 we must first look at Psalm 137. In Psalm 137, the psalmist sat and wept "by the rivers of Babylon" (v. 1). There, the captors and tormentors demanded songs from them, perhaps as a form of mockery or crude entertainment. God's people refused. "How can we sing the LORD's song on foreign soil?" (v. 4). They were far from the temple in Jerusalem, far from home. They paint for us a poignant picture of lyres hanging on the poplar trees by the waters of Babylon.

Has there been a season in your life when you could not sing? Explain. What prevented you from giving thanks to God in that season?

Here's the structure of Psalm 138:

1-3	David praising Yahweh for His character and His promises
4-5	The kings of the world hear Yahweh's word and praise Yahweh
6-8	David praising Yahweh for His character and His promises

REVIEW VERSES 1-3.

Psalm 138 is the response to the question in Psalm 137: "How can we sing?" God's people sang. They sang not to entertain their mockers and tormentors, but they sang to give thanks and praise to their true God. Before the false gods of Babylon, they worshiped Yahweh. Even on foreign soil, they sang a song of David, God's anointed king. They bowed toward Jerusalem.

What was the content of their song? His name and His Word. They sang about Yahweh's character: His faithfulness and truth (*emet*), His life-giving, unchanging, saving love (*hesed*). Unlike the gods made of metal and wood, Yahweh was the God who spoke and made covenants with His people. There is none like Him.

When David meditated on Yahweh's character and promises, his soul was made strong. As David deepened his understanding of who God is in accordance with God's word, his visible world conformed to the invisible reality of Yahweh. His faith grew in proportion to the depth of his understanding of God.

How does Yahweh's word and character strengthen you to give thanks today?

REVIEW VERSES 4-5. What prompted the kings to give thanks and what was the content of their song?

In giving thanks to God for Yahweh's name and His word, David was made strong in order to make known Yahweh's name and His word. In Psalm 2, the kings of the earth took their stand and conspired against Yahweh (v. 2). They were instructed to be wise and rejoice with trembling and worship the anointed King lest they perish in their rebellion (vv. 10-12).

Psalm 138 is a reversal of Psalm 2. Here in Book V, the kings of the earth gave thanks to Yahweh. The kings of the earth heard the promises (word) of Yahweh (name) and sang about Yahweh's ways and His great glory. Psalm 138 is also a reversal of Psalm 137. Captors and tormentors were demanding songs from God's people. In Psalm 138, the enemies were singing the songs of Zion.

REVIEW VERSES 6-7. What promises do we find in these verses?

Yahweh is full of grace! The humble and lowly call out to Yahweh, whose eyes look into the darkest places. Yahweh loves the lowly and disdains the haughty. He comes near the humble and despises the proud.

So ask for grace, and receive it. Ask for forgiveness, and receive it. We hate our weaknesses and foolishness. We hate that we have to face Satan, the world, and real enemies. But these things keep us going to God and asking the Lord for grace, strength, and forgiveness. They keep us humble and lowly. They keep us near Him.

REVIEW VERSE 8.

Verse 8 is a prayer. Here is my translation: "Yahweh, complete for me" or, "Yahweh, fulfill on my behalf." Most translations begin this verse as a declaration: "Yahweh will

This psalm ends with two requests: 1. Complete your faithful love on my behalf, and 2. Do not leave me! Stay with me in my deep dark well, now and forever, from exile to eternity. Here, I will give thanks, and kings will hear about you and will believe you. Kings will sing about your great glory. Fulfill your word in my life and demonstrate your character.

Yahweh's name and Yahweh's word are unchanging. We carry His name and His word no matter where we go.

> What does it mean to go in His name and with His word? Is that how you're approaching your walk of faith in this world? Explain.

Elisabeth Elliot wrote the book *Through Gates of Splendor*, the story of five young missionaries, including her husband Jim, who were martyred in their attempt to reach an isolated tribe in Ecuador with the gospel. The title of the book came from the song, *We Rest on Thee*, which Jim and his fellow missionaries sang together on the night before his death.[4]

> Close this day of study by meditating on the prayerful words of the third verse:

We go in faith, our own great weakness feeling,

and needing more each day thy grace to know:

yet from our hearts a song of triumph pealing,

"We rest on thee, and in thy name we go."[5]

WE REST ON THEE

Christ's GRATITUDE
AND CHRIST-LIKE
GRATITUDE

by Caroline Saunders

Sometimes in the Gospels, God the Son thanks God the Father, and honestly, it can feel a little strange. After all, though they are distinct from one another, they are both God. So, to our limited minds, gratitude within the Trinity can seem a little like, "Thanks, Me!"

In our confusion, it's tempting to rush past Jesus's gratitude to His Father, but let's slowly drink it in and consider how this can impact our own gratitude.

Throughout the Gospels, we see the Father and the Son gush about one another. Sometimes it's called praise and sometimes thankfulness, but these are varying shades of the same thing—pointing to God's goodness. Gratitude is pointing to God's goodness and making a big deal about it. For example, in Matthew 11:25, after reflecting on a particular quality of God the Father, Jesus exclaimed in delight, "I praise you, Father!" In other words, "I am so glad You're like this!" Or remember how God the Father reacted to Jesus's baptism? Jesus offered a picture of how He was going to obey the Father even unto death, and God the Father's delight spilled out from heaven: "This is my beloved Son, with whom I am well-pleased!" (Matt. 3:17). When the Father and the Son saw the other demonstrating God's character, they were ecstatic.

So, here's something to ponder: Who God is, is good news—even for God. And if God's character is good news for Him, how much more must it be good news for us!

> What characteristic of God feels like particularly good news for you today? Why?

Let's go back to that "I praise you, Father!" Jesus offered in Matthew 11, see what quality of God the Father provoked this splash of praise in Jesus, and discover how it can produce gratitude in us, too.

READ MATTHEW 11:25-26.

When we consider the book of Matthew as a whole, we can see what Jesus meant by "these things"—the upside-down kingdom God is building through Jesus.

What's the unexpected, "upside-down" part of this text? Why is this unexpectedness praise-worthy?

In His life, Jesus encountered many "wise and intelligent" religious leaders with wonky motivations. They said they desired to glorify God, but they were actually chasing their own glory. Characteristically, God didn't entrust Himself to those who cared about their own greatness and desired to lord it over others. Instead, He entrusted Himself to those who humbly acknowledged God's greatness, like the disciples.

Isn't it so "like God" to esteem the humility of a fisherman over the lofty intelligence of a trained scribe? Clearly, God's values are at odds with the world's values. This delighted Jesus, likely because He knew it all pointed to greater glory. For example, consider this moment in the early church: "When they observed the boldness of Peter and John and realized that they were *uneducated* and *untrained* men, they were amazed and *recognized that they had been with Jesus*" (Acts 4:13, emphasis added). The humility of God's people makes God's glory shine even brighter!

How would you describe God's unexpected, upside-down ways? How are you grateful for them?

When we see God's character, it produces gratitude in us—a substantive gratitude that can grow even in the most unexpected places. Paul modeled this powerfully in 2 Corinthians 12:7b-10.

> A thorn in the flesh was given to me, a messenger of Satan to
> torment me so that I would not exalt myself. Concerning this,
> I pleaded with the Lord three times that it would leave me. But
> he said to me, "My grace is sufficient for you, for my power is

perfected in weakness." Therefore, I will most gladly boast all the more about my weaknesses, so that Christ's power may reside in me. So I take pleasure in weaknesses, insults, hardships, persecutions, and in difficulties, for the sake of Christ. For when I am weak, then I am strong.

Circle any opposites you see in the text above. Then, in your own words, explain Paul's unexpected, upside-down gratitude.

Paul didn't invent this upside-down gratitude. He modeled it after Jesus!

READ MATTHEW 26:27-28. Scan the chapter to find the setting for this meal. Why is gratitude particularly upside-down and unexpected here?

When Jesus took a cup and gave thanks, it seemed like a simple act, but it was drenched with meaning. Consider these two ideas:

1. Throughout Scripture, a cup is used to symbolize God's wrath, which would be poured out on Jesus within hours of this prayer of gratitude.

2. Jesus called the cup His blood—a jarring description that must have echoed in the disciples' ears as they saw Jesus's blood poured out at His crucifixion.

How could Jesus give thanks for this cup?

Hebrews 12:2b helps us understand why Jesus could praise God for His suffering: "For the joy that lay before him, he endured the cross." Though the suffering itself would not be joyful, it would make the way for joy: God would receive glory, and God's family would be together with Him! All of it was a proclamation of God's character. He is so good!

> Make a list of similarities you see between Jesus's gratitude at the last supper and Paul's Christ-like gratitude in his suffering (2 Cor. 12:7b-10).

Sometimes we're tempted to use gratitude like a colorful bandage we stick on our wound, dismissively saying, "I'm fine! I have so much to be grateful for!" Yet in their gratitude, neither Jesus nor Paul denied their hardship.

> How is the unexpected gratitude of Jesus and Paul more substantial than optimism?

Even our most difficult trials are a means for God's glory and the building of God's family. Christ-like gratitude is never dismissive of our suffering; it's redemptive. How horrible would it be to suffer meaninglessly! Jesus's example teaches us that there is no meaningless suffering for those who follow the Lord.

It's easier to grasp this unexpected, upside-down view of suffering when we consider the opposites within our faith story.

Our limitless God took on the limitations of human flesh,

To die so that we might live,

So sinners could be made righteous,

So God's enemies could be made family,

So the humble could display God's glory.

Because of our unexpected, upside-down testimony, we can live with unexpected, upside-down gratitude. It's not a matter of clinging to fake optimism when times are tough; our faith is sturdier than that. Jesus's example shows us that gratitude is a response to God's character—character that never changes and is always good news for us.

Today you may be suffering, enduring the mundane, enjoying God's good gifts, or some combination of those three. Wherever you are, consider this: Where do you see God's goodness? How can you make a big deal about it, like Jesus did?

James 1:2-4 helps us see that even suffering is an opportunity for gratitude because suffering makes us more like Jesus and that is good news, always! Read the James passage and spend some time in prayer. Share your areas of suffering with God and ask Him to walk closely with you. Ask Him to redeem your places of difficulty into places of togetherness with Him. Ask God to help you know Him more. Ask Him to produce within you genuine, Christlike gratitude.

Gratitude PRODUCES GENEROSITY

by Cynthia Hopkins

Ten thousand miles. That's the distance scholars estimate the apostle Paul's missionary travels entailed.[6] For perspective, ten thousand miles is about the straight-line flight distance from Sydney, Australia to New York City—except Paul lived long before Orville and Wilbur Wright ever went airborne.[7] And his travels weren't a straight shot. Paul's ten thousand miles took place over land and sea with purposeful, extended layovers in at least fifty cities. It involved a span of about twenty six years (AD 35–61), in which Paul faced many dangers and sacrificed every physical comfort in service to God and people. (See 2 Cor. 11:23-28.)

Considering all of that, it's astounding to consider that Paul found the time to write thirteen New Testament letters. One time I forgot to send a birthday card to my best friend. I don't remember what busy activities in my life caused that oversight, but it probably aligned with my kid's select basketball season or season three of *Downton Abbey*. My point is, how did Paul find the margin? He didn't have a computer or even a typewriter or bottle of correction fluid. Why would he go to the trouble of writing letters of encouragement to so many people, many whom he had already encouraged in person? Hadn't he done enough?

There's an encounter in Luke 7:36-50 that helps us understand why. A Pharisee named Simon had invited Jesus over for dinner and thought that act of hospitality in and of itself was enough. But then a woman "who was a sinner" (v. 37) showed up and, in a broken mess of complete vulnerability, wept worshipfully as she washed Jesus's feet with her tears, dried them with her hair, and anointed them with her very expensive perfume. Simon had all kinds of questions about why that scene was taking place at his dinner party. So, Jesus told a story to teach Simon, and us, that true gratitude changes things. Jesus explained it plainly: "Her many sins have been forgiven; that's why she loved much. But the one who is forgiven little, loves little" (Luke 7:47). The simple fact is that Simon held back from Jesus; the woman did not.

GRATITUDE PRODUCES GENEROSITY

Like the woman at Simon's party, Paul didn't have to search to find the right time or reason to worship God. Knowing that his many sins had been forgiven, he loved much. That's why Paul traveled ten thousand miles over land and sea. It's why he sacrificed every physical comfort to preach the gospel. It's why, in his spare time, he wrote thirteen letters that make up a full third of the New Testament. Gratitude for the exceedingly generous gift of grace he had received in Christ compelled Paul to a lifestyle of worship, loving much, every moment of every day. As he did, other people also grabbed on to the wonder of life in Christ. When that happened, Paul didn't question it; he simply rejoiced.

GENEROSITY PRODUCES GRATITUDE

It's circular. In Paul's second letter to the Corinthians, we find a real life example of this. In 1 Corinthians 16, Paul had given the church instructions about collecting money for the needy church in Jerusalem. Evidently they had been eager to give at the outset, but it seems their interest had waned a bit. So, in 2 Corinthians 8–9 we find Paul urging them to finish what they started. He encouraged them to continue remembering the surpassing grace of God and allowing that grace to inform their actions. As they decided in their hearts to give generously to the work of ministry, they would produce thanksgiving to God in others (2 Cor. 9:6-14).

> What about you? Does God's generosity to you in Christ produce a lifestyle of ongoing generosity? If so, how? If not, why not?

> Is your relationship currency given freely or measured cautiously and carefully? Explain.

The depth of relationship Paul invested in people is something most women long for. We're grateful for it when we have it, and we're drawn to it when we see it. Think about Lucy and Ethel, Thelma and Louise, *The Sisterhood of the Traveling Pants*; those fictional characters are beloved because they exemplify our own capacity and desire for deep relationships with other women. We can become the very *best* friends! But it's also true that we often struggle to make those kind of friends. But why?

I think it's because we're usually waiting for someone else to take the first step. Many of us want to have deep friendships, but the initiative it takes to begin them makes us uncomfortable. We guard our hearts. We make assumptions. We're busy. We wrestle with insecurity. We keep our kindest thoughts private instead of verbalizing them because verbalizing them requires vulnerability, and vulnerability can end in disappointment. We are grateful and generous with some people sometimes, but a *generosity of spirit* is far less common among us.

When any of these realities exist in our hearts, the gratitude we experience is a squashed version. And God shows us the better way. Second Corinthians 9:6 is not a truth for finances only; it applies to the currencies of time, vulnerability, honesty, and love in all our relationships.

A grateful heart changes the way you relate to God and other people, and relating to God and other people generously will produce in you a more grateful heart.

You may not travel ten thousand actual miles to show your gratitude for God's gift of grace to you in Jesus Christ, but you can walk in the spirit of Paul's example. Look over these suggestions. Then choose a few to implement in your own life this week.

☐ Reframe your gratitude. Instead of saying, "Thank you," begin learning to say, "I thank God for you."

☐ The next time you're at a restaurant, give a generous tip and write an encouraging note to your server.

☐ Take someone you just met recently out to lunch or coffee (even if you're the "new" person in town!).

☐ Tell someone what God has been teaching you, and ask them to do the same.

☐ Send a card expressing thanks to someone who has been generous to you in some way.

☐ Write a note of gratitude for your mail carrier and/or leave a gift for them in the box.

☐ Write a letter of encouragement to someone going through a difficult circumstance.

☐ Leave a note of thanks or a small gift on top of the trash can for your sanitation workers.

☐ Give a gift of gratitude (like $5 gift cards to a favorite coffee shop) to church staff members.

☐ With family and friends, don't keep track of whose turn it is to call. If you haven't heard from someone in a while, go ahead and dial their number.

IT IS GOOD *to give thanks* TO THE LORD, TO SING PRAISE TO YOUR NAME, MOST HIGH.

Psalm 92:1

REFLECTION

As you finish your week of study, take a moment to process what you've learned and how your heart has been stirred concerning gratitude. Use the space below however you wish—write a prayer of thanks to the Lord, summarize what you've learned, write a poem, create a list of what you're grateful for, draw a picture, write a song, confess your struggle to be grateful, or document other expressions of your heart.

FOR THE GROUP TIME

If you're doing this study with a group, consider the following questions and be ready to discuss during your time together. (If you're leading the group, check out the leader guide at lifeway.com/grateful to help you prepare.)

Which day was your favorite day of study? Why?

What stood out to you from this week of personal study? What has stuck with you? What surprised you or was new information?

What's one thing you learned this week that will help you cultivate a heart of gratitude? How will you apply what you learned?

To continue developing and nurturing a heart of gratitude, get a copy of the *Gratitude Prayer Journal* at lifeway.com/grateful.

WEEK FOUR

GRATEFUL FOR GOD'S PROMISES

This week we will focus on how an understanding of God's promises, especially His promise to complete His work in us and in the world, motivates us to a life of thanksgiving and evangelism. We began our study by thinking about gratitude as a response to God's salvation and redemption, and this week we'll see the culmination of that in the promise of God's completed work in us. When we have this full picture, how could we not live every day out of gratitude to God for who He is and all He's done?

GOD *Keeps* HIS PROMISES

by Julie Busler

Strangers pressed in close on an overcrowded bus in a predominantly Muslim central Asian country. As most likely the only Christ follower in sight, I remember thinking "If this bus were to crash and all of us die, I would be the only one to go to heaven." Feelings reminiscent of survivor's guilt pierced my soul as the Lord made real to me, a new missionary, that death is a doorway into one of two eternal destinations.

That sudden sting of death was not new to me. I lost both of my parents, one from natural causes and one by their own hand, just prior to moving overseas. As devastating as those losses were, God used them to help me grasp that people are dying every day without hope in Christ.

But how do we keep going, trusting, and finding reasons to embrace a life of thanksgiving when faced with that grim reality? I believe we can find encouragement from the prophet Isaiah, whose book can be summed up in the meaning of his name: "Yahweh is salvation." Isaiah spoke a message on God's behalf to the leaders of Jerusalem and Judah, expressing God's judgment on Israel for their rebellion, breaking their covenant with God. But his announcement was tempered by a message of hope that is beautifully seen in chapter 25. These twelve verses are not only rich with reminders that God always keeps His promises, but they shift our gaze forward to our glorious, promised future.

READ ISAIAH 25:1-5.

Chapter 25 begins with a declaration of identity. Isaiah didn't say God is simply God, but said in verse one, "Lord you are *my* God" (emphasis mine). The God of Abraham, Isaac, and Jacob was Isaiah's God, and through faith in Christ, He is also your God. Even on the mission field, if others rejected the gospel and me along with it, I could count it all joy because I knew that no amount of earthly rejection could undo my belonging to God. Jesus, faithful and true, bought you to keep you. Gratitude often flows despite difficult circumstances when a child of God operates in the security of belonging we see promised throughout Scripture.

When you talk about or to God, do you refer to Him as "my God"?
Why or why not?

Describe how remembering you belong to God could foster gratitude when life is hard.

Isaiah then moves forward with intentional worship. He said: "I will exalt you. I will praise your name." The Hebrew word translated *praise* comes from "A verb meaning to acknowledge, to praise, to give thanks, to confess, to cast. The essential meaning is an act of acknowledging what is right about God in praise and thanksgiving."[1] And why did Isaiah praise God? Verse 1 says, "For you have accomplished wonders, plans formed long ago, with perfect faithfulness." Isaiah wasn't relying on his emotions to prompt his praise, but rather he decidedly worshiped the Lord from a place of thought and remembrance. Remembering that God keeps His promises grafted gratefulness into Isaiah's praise. If we skip ahead to Isaiah 46, we see God Himself say: "I declare the end from the beginning, and from long ago what is not yet done, saying: my plan will take place, and I will do all my will," (Isa. 46:10). When we remember His past faithfulness and keep our eyes on eternity, thankfulness becomes the natural response in the present.

When in your life has God proved faithful to keep His promises? How does that inspire gratefulness?

Upon praising his God, Isaiah declared that part of God's ancient plan was to turn the city into a pile of rock and ruins that would never be rebuilt so that a strong people will honor God. The city is not named, probably indicating it is symbolic, rather than specific.[2] Someday, ruthless cities, much like where I lived in central Asia, will turn toward God in belief. Heaven will overflow with worshipers who were formerly at war with God and His people. Remembering this has spurred me on in sharing Jesus with others. But the driving force behind every evangelism effort must be hope. Not merely wishful thinking, but rather, an expectation that God will do what He has promised. He has always been and will always be a stronghold and refuge for His afflicted saints. Any earthly trial is fertile ground for gratitude to grow when you intentionally reflect on the goodness and faithfulness of God like Isaiah did.

Have you ever felt discouraged when you shared Christ with others? Explain.

How is biblical hope different from worldly hope? How can biblical hope help you remain grateful when your evangelism efforts don't immediately appear fruitful?

READ ISAIAH 25:6-9.

There's a thread of sorrow woven throughout my story, both from personal losses as well as sadness over friends who have yet to accept Jesus as Lord. Even Jesus wept in the face of death with heartfelt sorrow (John 11:35), indicating sorrow over death does not mean a lack of faith. Tears are part of the human experience, but what I love about verses 6-9 is that they give us a glimpse of the coming joy that has been promised. The way Isaiah feasted his mind on this eschatological celebration in Zion is worthy of our imitation. This large mountaintop feast will be attended by people from every race, nation, and language. The veil of death and sorrow that has shaded life since sin entered the world in Eden, will be destroyed. The Hebrew word translated *swallow up* paints the powerful picture of death being defeated forever. "God uncovers the face of the corpse and speaks the word of resurrection, removing the disgrace of his people from the whole earth. They rise in power, never to die again. The disgrace of sin and death has been swallowed up in victory." (1 Cor. 15:54).³ God's redemption plan is on a worldwide scale, yet it is also personal.

One day, the Lord will wipe away your last tear. On that day, we will join with others from every nation with rejoicing and gladness saying "Look, this is our God; we have waited for him, and he has saved us" (v. 9).

Describe a time when you felt sorrow over the death of a loved one.

How does knowing death will be swallowed up help you be grateful despite the present sting of death?

READ ISAIAH 25:10-12.

While the end of the chapter may seem odd at first glance, it provides infinite comfort that inspires endurance while we wait for our glorious future with Him. Many believe Moab represents those who will never believe God. Part of the unending joy in eternity for believers comes from God weeding out every thing or person that causes sin and does evil. Because we can trust God to keep His promises, we can know for certain that we will dwell in peace and safety in a place where the arrogant will no longer assault. I am so grateful for this certain future that is mine through Christ. Even if my heart shatters under the sting of death while bound on this earth, someday there will be nothing but the glorious shine of joy, and for that I am grateful.

Grateful FOR THE ENDING

by Elizabeth Hyndman

'm not really a future-focused person. I like to think about some what-ifs and daydream a little, but I don't have a five-year plan, goals for the next year, or any idea what I might eat for dinner tonight. It's not that I don't have ambitions in life. In job interviews, I used to answer that typical ten-year plan question with a quip about God always messing up my plans. I'd say it jokingly, but it's true. I never thought my life would look the way it does now.

> What about you? Are you a future planner? Does your life look like you thought it would? Explain.

Based on the anecdotal evidence of observing most people I know, I would venture to guess that you answered no to that last question. James 4:13a provides a scriptural basis for your answer: "Yet you do not know what tomorrow will bring—what your life will be!" After all, as Proverbs 16:9 says, "A person's heart plans his way, but the LORD determines his steps."

There's a lot we don't know about the future. However, we do know the most important thing about it—death is defeated.

SKIM 1 CORINTHIANS 15. It's a lot of verses, but if you read it out loud, I bet you'll be fired up by the end of it. There might even be an "Amen!"

> Which of the verses, if any, stood out to you? Did any of what you just read raise questions in your mind? If so, jot those down.

It's okay to sit with questions. Even in these very verses, Paul stated that he's telling us "a mystery" (v. 51).

Essentially, this entire chapter is talking about Jesus's resurrection from the dead. The Corinthian believers had started to doubt the resurrection. They were most likely influenced by the Greek culture around them who had no trouble believing in some kind of spiritual after-death existence, but not a bodily resurrection.[4] Paul was passionately arguing that Christ was raised bodily, and so would we!

READ VERSE 19 AGAIN. Rewrite it in your own words.

This week, we're talking about being grateful for God's promises, especially His promise to complete His work in us and in the world. Verse 19 speaks to a promise for the future, but it has implications for our present.

If we put our hope in Christ only for this life, we are to be pitied. Yes, Jesus came to give us life in abundance in the here and now (John 10:10), but our hope is for a future day when we will experience life everlasting in His presence. The way we live in that hope in the present cultivates both gratitude and evangelism.

READ VERSES 54-57 AGAIN. Does the language Paul used here sound familiar?

Paul is using language ("swallowed up") you read yesterday in Isaiah 25:7, as well as language found in Hosea 13:14, "Death, where are your barbs? Sheol, where is your sting?"

What does Christ give us victory over?

The entire chapter culminates in these verses. The Corinthian believers doubted resurrection; Paul made the case that without resurrection, the gospel was null and void. To make his case, Paul looked back at the first man, Adam (1 Cor. 15:45-49).

What do you know about the story of Adam and Eve?

Why did God tell Adam in Genesis 2:16-17 to not eat from the tree of the knowledge of good and evil?

LOOK AT GENESIS 3:19,22. What was one of the consequences of disobedience for Adam and Eve?

The rest of the Bible is filled with lists of names. Many are punctuated by the phrase, "then he died." The consequence of sin is death.

The Corinthians weren't doubting they would die. They were doubting their future resurrection. Paul said that to doubt our own resurrections is to doubt Christ's. And, as verse 17 says, "if Christ has not been raised, your faith is worthless" Death has not been defeated. Christ has been proven a liar. And we are still in our sins. BUT, as Paul clearly states in verse 20, "Christ has been raised from the dead." Not only that, He is the "firstfruits." Firstfruits was an Old Testament ritual where the first part of the harvest was dedicated to God and also indicated more harvest would follow.[5] Jesus's resurrection was first. We are the more to follow!

Jesus died on the cross for our sins. But it's because He was resurrected three days later that we have hope. The CSB Study Bible puts it beautifully, "[Christ's resurrection] is God's 'amen' to Christ's 'it is finished.'"[6]

Write a short prayer of thanks to God for the gift of eternal life and the victory He has given us through Jesus.

READ 1 CORINTHIANS 15:58. What is the "therefore" there for?

This verse is the action plan, the next steps, and the way in which the information we just read should impact our everyday lives.

What three things does Paul tell the Corinthians to do in light of the resurrection?

LOOK BACK AT VERSES 1-2. Why do you think Paul used words and phrases like "taken your stand," "immovable," "steadfast," and "hold to" when referring to the gospel and the resurrection?

Have you ever had to be "steadfast" or "immovable" regarding your beliefs? What did that look like for you?

Paul addressed this letter in a time and to a church where the doctrine of the resurrection was in question. In our culture today, doctrines are in question, as well. As the world around us—and even some in the church—question the truth of Scripture, we must hold fast to the gospel. We must be immovable.

> How does holding to the truth of the gospel and God's promise of victory stir up gratitude in your heart and mind?

The truth that we will one day be resurrected with Christ is a mystery, to borrow Paul's word. There are a lot of details about that future hope that are unknown to us. We can't comprehend how beautiful, how gracious, how lovely that will be. Our finite brains cannot grasp infinity. We don't know exactly what our resurrected bodies will look like. And only God knows when the trumpet will sound and "we will be changed" (v. 52).

What we do know for certain, though, is "that Christ died for our sins according to the Scriptures, that he was buried, that he was raised on the third day according to the Scriptures" (vv. 3-4), and that God "gives us the victory through our Lord Jesus Christ!" (v. 57).

And for that we can be grateful. Forever and ever.

HIS *Speaking* IS HIS DOING

by Irene Sun

Younger women often ask me, "Who should I marry?" My answer is always "A man of integrity." When you are young and in love with love, the concept of integrity is not very exciting. But integrity is the foundation of any relationship of trust. A man of integrity is consistent and undivided in word and works.

When he tells you he values purity, does he keep his word?
When he tells you he loves his parents, does he keep his word?
Is there a pattern of lying, making excuses, not being true to his words?
Are his words measured and honest and true?
Does he keep his promises?
Does he admit his shortcomings?
Does he apologize without giving excuses?
Does he blame others for his mistakes?
Does he confess sin and ask for forgiveness?

All of us who follow Christ should seek to live with this lofty standard of integrity. But here is the devastating truth—even with our best effort and most sincere intention, human words and actions fail. Every single person that ever walked the earth is unable to live lives of perfect integrity. We are all hypocrites and liars, except for One.

READ PSALM 33.

VERSES 1-3

The first line of Psalm 33 is firmly sewn to the last line of Psalm 32. The English translations loosen this seam, sadly. In the original Hebrew text, the last verse of Psalm 32 and the first verse of Psalm 33 exhort the righteous ones (*tsadiqim*) to shout for joy (*ranan*).[7]

Psalm 33 is the song of the forgiven. In Psalm 32, David cried out to Yahweh to confess his sin and the weight of his transgression. Yahweh was his hiding place, and God's faithful love surrounded David. What made the new song new in Psalm 33:3? It was a song overflowing from a new heart.

Psalm 33 was the song of one who was delivered, the shout of joy of a person who was forgiven. When we are in sin, we have no words in our mouths. We are like the beast of the field, with no understanding (32:9). But praise, joy, and thanksgiving pour out of the lips of those who are forgiven!

VERSES 4-9

When was a time your words or your lack of words hurt others?

Human words hurt and destroy. God's Word creates.

Human words are inadequate. God's Word is sufficient.

Human words fail. God's Word is faithful and true.

"For the word of the Yahweh is right, and all his work is trustworthy" (33:4). The word *trustworthy* or *emet* also means *faithful and true*.[8] When Jesus, who is the Word made flesh, comes again, the name He comes in is Faithful and True (Rev. 19:11).

> *For the word of the Yahweh is right, and all his work is trustworthy.*
>
> **PSALM 33:4**

Human words are inadequate. In the face of great trouble or tragedy, we might say, "I don't know what to say," or "I have no words." Our words cannot make things right. Our words are hollow and fall short of what is required.

But Yahweh is all-powerful, all-loving, all-knowing. All of his words are all-powerful, all-loving, all-knowing. What He says is done. He possesses infinite integrity in His words and His works. His speaking is His doing. He spoke the world into being. He gathers the water with His words. He formed the galaxies with His breath.

Behold, this is our God! Faithful and True! We give thanks and we bow down in worship.

VERSES 10-19

While the nations and kingdoms of the world rise and fall, Yahweh's counsel stands forever. Kings and rulers may make plans, but Yahweh is the Sovereign who has the power to make and break. Therefore, the nation whose God is Yahweh is blessed. His people are His treasured possession. We are not our own; we belong to God.

What are the different ways the CSB describes Yahweh's seeing in verses 13-19?

Human attention is fleeting, brief, limited, and weak. Human attention is easily distracted, diverted, and disturbed.

In His infinite kindness and with His infinite knowledge, Yahweh looks down from heaven. He attends to the work of our hands and the intention of our hearts. His gaze is focused, never distracted, diverted, or disturbed. He observes every person. Not one person, not kings nor warriors, no detail escapes His understanding.

Whom we behold determines how we behave. We keep our eyes on Yahweh who keeps His eyes on those who fear Him. His eyes stay on those who depend on His faithful love.

What does it mean to fear Yahweh?

In the context of Psalm 33, those who fear Yahweh are those who put their hope on His character and trust in His promises. If He promises He forgives, trust that He has forgiven. If He promises He will rescue, we trust that He will rescue.

Fearing Yahweh is to focus our minds and hearts on Him, staying our affection and attention on Him who is unseen.

His speaking and His seeing is our comfort and confidence. The One who sees all things is also the One who rules over all things. In trouble and danger, we need not fear. Even when we are unable to see Him, He sees us. He promises to rescue us and to keep us alive.

VERSES 20-22

Waiting is the discipline of depending on Yahweh's word, promises, and counsel from moment to moment. In waiting, we bend our minds and hearts to attend and focus on our invisible God, by hoping and trusting on His visible word.

So we keep His Word and His works before our eyes. We keep our gaze and attention on "whatever is true, whatever is honorable, whatever is just, whatever is pure, whatever is lovely, whatever is commendable—if there is any moral excellence and if there is anything praiseworthy—dwell on these things" (Phil. 4:8). We also consider the visible examples of God's work and word set before us as we observe saints who live out faithful lives for the sake of Christ.

With the psalmist, we call out to Yahweh and ask that He would rest His hesed on us. He saved us in the past; He saves us now; He will save us again. "May your faithful love rest on us, LORD, for we put our hope in you" (v. 22).

> Write down some visible examples of God's work and Word you want to keep your eyes on today.

Forever GRATEFUL

by Y Bonesteele

oneliness is something we all experience in certain seasons of our lives. We all want a sense of belonging and purpose and when we don't have those things, it's easy to think that we are alone. But the Bible tells us we are never alone. Because not only is God always with us, we belong in His family and kingdom and our purpose is to worship and serve Him. And this isn't just for a season; it's for an eternity.

God's plan throughout Scripture has always been to bring His people together in His presence that He may love and protect and provide for us. And because we always fail to live up to His holiness, He provided a way through His Son, Jesus. God's plan and promise are to redeem mankind and establish His kingdom for all tongues, tribes, and nations. In Revelation 7, we see a glimpse of what this ultimate plan will look like.

READ REVELATION 7:9-17. THEN READ VERSES 9-10 AGAIN.

How did John, the author, describe this multitude of people?

What are they acknowledging about God?

In Revelation 7:9, John saw a large crowd from every nation standing before the throne of God. This vision confirms that God's promise to bring both Jew and Gentile to Himself will be completed. We will stand before the Lord Christ Jesus, the Lamb, clothed in white robes and with palm branches. The white robes symbolize the purity and sinlessness that we have been longing for and the palm branches symbolize our acknowledgment of Christ's victory over sin, death, guilt, shame, and suffering. We will worship God, crying out, "Salvation belongs to our God!" We will cry in one voice, as one people of God, because Christ has finished what He set out to do—save His people. Save His people from death, but also save them to that ultimate reality of belonging.

How amazing that day will be—to be so unified in His presence in worship! We will fully understand that we are not alone. We will belong to the fellowship of believers from every tribe and nation! Currently, we don't see this unity and we don't always feel that we belong; the world seems chaotic with many of us trying to find our own way. But here, God promises that one day, everything will change. It would be easy to focus on our current situation, but the Spirit reminds us of His promises and stirs our hearts to be grateful in anticipation of that day before God's throne, knowing in confidence that it will come.

> How should we focus our prayers for more unity in the world knowing that one day all who believe will come together as one before God?

It takes a lot of grace and listening to find common ground and be unified with those who have differing views. But when we focus on the essentials, we find ourselves more unified than we think! When we put Christ first, and focus on His saving work, we will find ourselves drawing closer to our fellow brothers and sisters as well as drawing closer to Him. When we thank God for fellow believers, we find ourselves grateful for that blessed day to come when we all will be in His throne room.

> **READ REVELATION 7:11-12 AGAIN.** What attributes are the angels, elders, and creatures bestowing on God? Which of these attributes do you resonate most with when you think about God and why?

Because God is the Creator of all things, He deserves worship from all His creation. At the end of days, the angels, the elders, the four living creatures, and all His people will worship. Though we don't know exactly what these particular beings are, what's important is that they are praising God, falling facedown, acknowledging His greatness with reverence and awe. They aren't giving God these things; they are proclaiming the glory and honor due to Him.

How can your worship of God be more like that of these creatures?

Because sometimes we see God as a Friend or Father, we can come to Him nonchalantly, presenting our requests and prayers. This isn't wrong, but sometimes we forget the magnitude of who He is and forget the fear and trembling that is due. May we come to Him in familiarity and effortlessness, but may we also come to Him in reverence and awe, knowing He is all-powerful and has done great things!

READ REVELATION 7:13-17. Who are those robed in white, and what is their role?

What will God do for them?

In John's vision, one of the elders rhetorically asked him, "Who are these people in white robes and where did they come from? John responded, "Sir, you know." The elder then answered his own question by describing them as those who came out of the great tribulation—the time of suffering associated with the end times (Dan. 12:1-3; Matt. 24:15-28). There are differing views on the specifics of this tribulation, but the main point here is that these white robed people have come out of it and are now before God's throne. How? By washing their robes in the blood of the Lamb. They accepted Jesus's sacrifice as an atonement for their sins and received Christ as Lord. Thus, their past has led them to the present scene.

Throughout this passage, John repeats the words "before," "throne," "God," and "Lamb." His emphasis is that as believers, we are given the right to be in God's presence, in the presence of Christ the Lamb, to be before His throne forevermore. When we fully consider this, how can we not be grateful?

But there's more! The elder then described how God will protect, provide for, guide, and bring joy to our lives forevermore. We will no longer hunger or thirst or need air conditioning or be uncomfortable or feel wayward, lost, anxious, or sad. John's vision was prophetic and a promise from the Lord. He was encouraging those in the early church to remember that though they were suffering, this day of glory would come. Christ will return and all those who have trusted in Him will be with Him forever in His kingdom.

> **How does this truth make you grateful for who God is and what His ultimate mission is?**

Sometimes it's difficult to be grateful, especially when life seems overwhelming. But also in our day-to-day repetitious living, we become complacent and neglect to offer thanks. Even when things are going well, sometimes we focus on earthly "blessings" and find most of our gratefulness pointed toward things that will soon fade away.

However, when we meditate on God's promises of His forever kingdom with a unified, diverse people, of His forever glory and presence with us, and of His forever provision and protection, our spirits can do nothing less than worship and be thankful. A day is coming when we, with all tribes and nations, will weep no more. God has promised it, and He always keeps His promises. That's something we can be forever grateful for.

> **What other promises of God from Scripture can you list and thank God for?**

Gratitude
MOTIVATES
MISSION

by Cynthia Hopkins

Dumbstruck. That's how I imagine the disciples in Acts 1:10 as they watched Jesus ascend into heaven. What a rush of conflicting emotions they must have felt! They were probably anxious and scared to see Jesus leaving them, but also filled with hope and anticipation to know His Spirit would come. It's likely they were confused about questions Jesus seemed to have left unanswered, while being grateful for all they had seen, experienced, and learned. They weren't sure where to go or what to do, yet they knew they would step forward in purpose and power.

But in that moment, they couldn't step forward. In fact, they couldn't move or utter a single word. All they could do was stare at the sky.

Can you relate? Sometimes life hits especially hard. We know that Jesus has saved us, is with us, and is working in us. We trust in His promises and understand that He has called us to join His mission in the world. But difficult circumstances leave us feeling paralyzed and dumbstruck.

How are you supposed to step forward in God's mission and practice gratitude when personal pain and loss seems to necessitate your full attention? Does God even expect you to?

God knew the disciples would struggle to reconcile the wild range of emotions they were feeling when Jesus's feet left earth and rose to the throne room of heaven. He knew we would struggle, too. He knew there would be times when we would be tempted to push aside gratitude and sit firmly in our grief. For the disciples, He sent a couple of angels to remind them, and now us, to fix our eyes on the overarching truth. Life on earth is short. Jesus will return, and He will supplant the painful ponderings of earth with a painless and glorious reality—for *eternity*.

That is not to say that questions and confusion and grief are, in and of themselves, sinful. They are not! Jesus experienced those emotions Himself, like when His friend Lazarus died (John 11:35), and when He pondered the suffering He would face at the cross (Luke 22:39-46). But in those experiences, He kept looking forward to the bigger, better gospel truth that compelled His coming to earth in the first place. Every day Jesus had on earth, He kept stepping forward to fulfill God's kingdom purposes. And so must we.

We've learned this week that gratitude motivates mission, so step into that truth with today's exercise. Around the word *grief*, write as many things as you can that you have grieved, are now grieving, and will one day likely grieve.

Grief

Around the word *gratitude*, write as many things as you can that you are grateful for. (Think about who God is, the big and small things He has done for you, what He is doing, and what He has promised.)

Gratitude

Consider both lists in prayer before God. Invite Him to help you begin to see your grief in light of your gratitude so that you might begin to step forward on mission in every circumstance.

GIVE THANKS
in everything;
FOR THIS IS GOD'S WILL FOR YOU IN CHRIST JESUS.

1 Thessalonians 5:18

REFLECTION

As you finish your week of study, take a moment to process what you've learned and how your heart has been stirred concerning gratitude. Use the space below however you wish—write a prayer of thanks to the Lord, summarize what you've learned, write a poem, create a list of what you're grateful for, draw a picture, write a song, confess your struggle to be grateful, or document other expressions of your heart.

FOR THE GROUP TIME

If you're doing this study with a group, consider the following questions and be ready to discuss during your time together. (If you're leading the group, check out the leader guide at lifeway.com/grateful to help you prepare.)

Which day was your favorite day of study? Why?

What stood out to you from this week of personal study? What has stuck with you? What surprised you or was new information?

What's one thing you learned this week that will help you cultivate a heart of gratitude? How will you apply what you learned?

To continue developing and nurturing a heart of gratitude, get a copy of the *Gratitude Prayer Journal* at lifeway.com/grateful.

ENDNOTES

INTRODUCTION

1. "Giving Thanks Can Make You Happier," *Harvard Health Publishing*, August 14, 2021, https://www.health.harvard.edu/healthbeat/giving-thanks-can-make-you-happier.

WEEK ONE

1. Louis Berkhof, *Systematic Theology*, (Louisville, KY: GLH Publishing, 2022), 67.

2. John H. Sammis, "Trust and Obey," *Baptist Hymnal* (Nashville: Convention Press, 1991), 447.

3. John MacArthur, *Luke 11–17, MacArthur New Testament Commentary* (Chicago, IL: Moody Publishers, 2013), 394.

4. Strong's G509: *anōthen*, Blue Letter Bible, accessed March 13, 2023, https://www.blueletterbible.org/lexicon/g509/csb/mgnt/0-1/.

5. Sarah E. Fisher, "Khesed—Loyal Love in Action," *Hebrew Word Lessons*, October 22, 2017, https://hebrewwordlessons.com/2017/10/22/chesed-an-action-packed-word-without-translation/.

6. Psalm 136:1, CSB, Blue Letter Bible, accessed April 10, 2023, https://www.blueletterbible.org/csb/psa/136/1/t_cPonc_614001.

7. Klyne Snodgrass, *Ephesians, The NIV Application Commentary* (Grand Rapids, MI: Zondervan, 1996), 102.

8. Strong's G5485: *charis*, Blue Letter Bible, accessed March 13, 2023, https://www.blueletterbible.org/lexicon/g5485/csb/mgnt/0-1/.

9. Max Anders, *Galatians-Colossians, vol. 8, Holman New Testament Commentary* (Nashville, TN: Broadman & Holman Publishers, 1999), 112.

10. Klyne Snodgrass, *Ephesians, The NIV Application Commentary* (Grand Rapids, MI: Zondervan, 1996), 104.

WEEK TWO

1. David Guzik, *1 Samuel, David Guzik's Commentaries on the Bible* (Santa Barbara, CA: David Guzik, 2013), 1 Sa 4:3–4.

2. "What is significant about the Ark of the Covenant? What is it?" *Compelling Truth*, Accessed March 13, 2023, https://www.compellingtruth.org/What-Ark-of-the-Covenant.html.

3. Gregory Brown, "The Clothing Of The Heavenly Citizen (Colossians 3:5-14)," January 25, 2016, Bible.org, https://bible.org/seriespage/11-clothing-heavenly-citizen-colossians-35-14.

4. "Compassion," *Merriam-Webster.com Dictionary*, accessed March 13, 2023, https://www.merriam-webster.com/dictionary/compassion.

5. Laura Story, "Blessings," *Blessings* Album, 2011.

WEEK THREE

1. Tony Evans, "Acts 16:16-18," *The Tony Evans Bible Commentary* (Nashville: Holman Bible Publishers, 2019), 1095.

2. John Polhill, "Acts 16:37," *The ESV Study Bible* (Wheaton, IL: Crossway, 2008), 2120.

3. John Polhill, "Acts 12:18-19," *The ESV Study Bible* (Wheaton, IL: Crossway, 2008), 2108.

4. Elisabeth Elliot, "Hymns: We Rest on Thee / It is Well," *Gateway to Joy broadcast*, September 5, 1990, https://elisabethelliot. org/resource-library/gateway-to-joy/ hymns-we-rest-on-thee-it-is-well/.

5. Edith G. Cherry, "We Rest on Thee," 1895.

6. "Paul," *The Roman Empire, PBS.org*, Accessed March 13, 2023, https://www.pbs.org/empires/ romans/empire/paul.html.

7. David Slotnik, "I flew on Qantas' 'Project Sunrise,' a nonstop flight from New York to Sydney. . . , " *Business Insider*, October 21, 2019, https://www.businessinsider.com/ qantas-longest-flight-new-york-sydney-project- sunrise-review-pictures-2019-10.

WEEK FOUR

1. Warren Baker, Eugene Carpenter, *The Complete Word Study Dictionary: Old Testament* (Chattanooga, TN: AMG Publishers, 2003), 419.

2. Gary V. Smith, *Isaiah 1–39, ed. E. Ray Clendenen, The New American Commentary* (Nashville: B&H Publishing Group, 2007), 430.

3. Andrew M. Davis, *Christ-Centered Exposition: Exalting Jesus in Isaiah* (Nashville: B&H Publishing Group, 2017), 146.

4. Mark Taylor, *1 Corinthians, ed. E. Ray Clendenen, vol. 28, The New American Commentary* (Nashville, TN: B&H Publishing Group, 2014), 367.

5. Richard L. Pratt Jr, *I & II Corinthians, vol. 7, Holman New Testament Commentary* (Nashville, TN: Broadman & Holman Publishers, 2000), 287.

6. F. Alan Tomlinson, *CSB Study Bible Notes* (Nashville: Holman Bible Publishers, 2017), 1832.

7. Strong's H6662: *sadîq*, Blue Letter Bible, accessed March 13, 2023, https://www. blueletterbible.org/lexicon/h6662/csb/ wlc/0-1/. Strong's H7442: *rānan*, Blue Letter Bible, accessed March 13, 2023, https://www. blueletterbible.org/lexicon/h7442/csb/wlc/0-1/.

8. Strong's H530: *'ĕmûnâ*, Blue Letter Bible, accessed March 13, 2023, https://www. blueletterbible.org/lexicon/h530/csb/wlc/0-1/.

CONTRIBUTORS

WENDY BELLO

Wendy Bello is an author and Bible teacher. She was born in Cuba, but now lives in Miami, Florida. A frequent speaker at conferences and retreats around the country and internationally, she is passionate about teaching women the Word of God so they can live grounded in it. She is the author of several books including *Más allá de mi lista de oración* (*Beyond my Prayer List*), *Digno* (*Worthy*) and *Un corazón nuevo* (*A New Heart*). Wendy and her husband, Abel, have two children.

Y BONESTEELE

Y Bonesteele is the content editor of *The Gospel Project* Adult Bible Study curriculum and is a former missionary to Spain. She has her MDiv from Talbot School of Theology with an emphasis in Discipleship and Evangelism and enjoys gardening, siestas, and coffee with her vanilla creamer. She also enjoys traveling with her four kids and one husband.

JULIE BUSLER

Julie Busler is currently serving as the Oklahoma President of WMU. While she loves teaching Scripture as a whole, she often uses her experiences alongside Scripture to teach how to thrive despite mental illness. Julie and Ryan have been married sixteen years, have four children, and have served overseas as missionaries in Canada, Mexico, Germany, and Turkey. Her book, *Joyful Sorrow: Breaking Through the Darkness of Mental Illness,* is available where books are sold online.

ERIN FRANKLIN

Erin Franklin is a production editor on the Lifeway Women Bible Studies team. A graduate of Lipscomb University, she enjoys a good ping-pong match, photography, and learning new things. You can connect with her on Instagram @erin_franklin and on Twitter @erinefranklin.

JANICE GAINES

Janice Gaines is a Stellar and Dove Award-nominated recording artist and speaker. A seminary graduate with a Masters of Divinity, she is a sought-after teacher with a passion for seeing people reconciled to God, and to each other. Janice is a mom to two boys and co-hosts the *Only Gaines* podcast with her husband, EJ Gaines.

CYNTHIA HOPKINS

Cynthia Hopkins is a longtime writer of Bible studies, devotions, and articles across all age groups from students through senior adults. She now serves in that capacity on Lifeway's custom content and short term studies team—remotely from The Woodlands, Texas. Cynthia is exceedingly grateful for that work and the many other ways God shows Himself to her!

ELIZABETH HYNDMAN

Elizabeth Hyndman is the editorial project leader for Lifeway Women Academy and cohosts the *MARKED* podcast. A Nashville native, grammarian, and tea drinker, Elizabeth can be found on Instagram and Twitter @edhyndman.

RAVIN MCKELVY

Ravin McKelvy is a copywriter at Lifeway and graduated with a degree in communications from Moody Bible Institute. She is passionate about the intersection of art and theology and sharing the daily realities of Christian living on social media.

TESSA MORRELL

Tessa Morrell is a production editor for Lifeway Women. She is passionate about serving in her church and studying Scripture with others. She also enjoys visiting local coffee shops, browsing antique stores for hours, and creating art of all kinds.

APRIL RODGERS

April Rodgers is the published author of *Made to Shine: 90 Devotions to Enjoy and Reflect God's Light*. After losing her brother in a tragic car accident, April held on to her faith in God and allowed Him to turn her darkness into light. Now she lives to encourage others to shine in their everyday lives by speaking at conferences and shining God's light on her YouTube® channel titled "The Reflecting Light Show." April is a seminary graduate with her Masters of Theological Studies, wife to an amazing man, and mom to two sweet daughters. Her favorite things consist of coffee, community, and Sunday afternoon naps. You can visit her website at aprilrodgers.com.

CONTRIBUTORS

CAROLINE SAUNDERS

Caroline Saunders is a writer, Bible teacher, pastor's wife, and mother of three who believes in taking Jesus seriously and being un-serious about nearly everything else. She's written two Bible studies for teen girls with Lifeway Girls (*Good News: How to Know the Gospel and Live It* and *Better Than Life: How to Study the Bible and Like It*), a retelling of the books of Joel, Amos, and Jonah for elementary readers called *Sound the Alarm*, and two picture books for kids (*The Story of Water* and *The Story of Home*, B&H Kids). Find her writing, resources, and ridiculousness at writercaroline.com, on Instagram @writercaroline, and on TikTok @writercarolinesaunders.

IRENE SUN

Irene Sun was born in Malaysia and is the author of the picture books *Taste and See: All About God's Goodness* and *God Counts: Numbers in His Word and His World*. She studied liturgy and literature at Yale University (MAR) and Old Testament and Semitic Languages at Trinity Evangelical Divinity School (ThM). She now teaches her four boys at home with her preacher husband, Hans. They serve and belong to Pittsburgh Chinese Church.

EMILY WICKHAM

Emily Wickham is passionate about sharing God's Word. As an award-winning writer, author, speaker, and ministry founder, she reaches many with biblical truths. Mark's wife for over thirty three years, mother of four adult children, and mother-in-love of two, Emily lives in western North Carolina. Please connect with her at proclaiminghimtowomen.com.

CHRISTINA ZIMMERMAN

Christina Zimmerman is enjoying retirement after serving as the content editor for the *YOU* Bible Study at Lifeway Christian Resources. She serves in ministry with her husband, Harry Zimmerman Jr., at Faith United Baptist Church, Nashville. They have five children.

BECOMING A CHRISTIAN

Romans 10:17 says, "So faith comes from what is heard, and what is heard comes through the message about Christ."

Maybe you've stumbled across new information in this study. Or maybe you've attended church all your life, but something you read here struck you differently than it ever has before. If you have never accepted Christ but would like to, read on to discover how you can become a Christian.

Your heart tends to run from God and rebel against Him. The Bible calls this sin. Romans 3:23 says, "For all have sinned and fall short of the glory of God."

Yet God loves you and wants to save you from sin, to offer you a new life of hope. John 10:10b says, "I have come so that they may have life and have it in abundance."

To give you this gift of salvation, God made a way through His Son, Jesus Christ. Romans 5:8 says, "But God proves his own love for us in that while we were still sinners, Christ died for us."

You receive this gift by faith alone. Ephesians 2:8-9 says, "For you are saved by grace through faith, and this not from yourselves; it is God's gift—not from works, so that no one can boast."

Faith is a decision of your heart demonstrated by the actions of your life. Romans 10:9 says, "If you confess with your mouth, 'Jesus is Lord,' and believe in your heart that God raised him from the dead, you will be saved."

If you trust that Jesus died for your sins and want to receive new life through Him, pray a prayer similar to the following to express your repentance and faith in Him:

Dear God, I know I am a sinner. I believe Jesus died to forgive me of my sins. I accept Your offer of eternal life. Thank You for forgiving me of all my sins. Thank You for my new life. From this day forward, I will choose to follow You.

If you have trusted Jesus for salvation, please share your decision with your group leader or another Christian friend. If you are not already attending church, find one in which you can worship and grow in your faith. Following Christ's example, ask to be baptized as a public expression of your faith.